Will My Beagle Go With Me in The Rapture?

Hope of Heaven for Dog Lovers and Their Pets

By Don Diehl

Sadie and Don

ii.

PROLOGUE

At the very get-go let me answer the question raised in the title of this book: "Will My Beagle Go With Me In The Rapture?" The answer is "yes." Admittedly I am being cautiously "dog"matic (if one can be cautious and dogmatic at the same time). There is a lot here to unpack, but yes, I believe that if I am alive and my beloved Beagle "Sadie" is alive when Jesus Christ comes a second time* the two of us (along with a lot of others) will be "caught up" together to meet the Lord in the air and be ushered into Heaven.

I knew I had to get all of that said fast. These ideas can be pretty dog gone arguable. So Sadie and I will spend the remainder of these pages to present our case — not just about eschatology [study of final things, particularly the destiny of the soul], but about the real issues of life — here and now life, and eternal life.

What is asked of the reader is that you consider these thoughts as more than just fanciful. It is by imagination that the author hears his pooch speak yet I am confident that communication does take place between humans and the creatures they call pets. If there was audible conversation or telepathy,** I imagine it would unfold about the way I am presenting it in this book. In a sense I am speaking for the Beagle. As her "Loving Master," she gives me permission to do that . . . and to speak for myself as well.

---

*"So Christ was once offered to bear the sins of many; and unto them that look for him shall he appear the second time without sin unto salvation." — Hebrews 9:28. **telepathy | təˌlepəTHē | noun — the supposed communication of thoughts or ideas by means other than the known senses.

INTRODUCTION:

I have spent my life as a working and sometimes skeptical journalist. From my own small town weekly newspaper to one of the largest daily newspapers in the Southwest (The Daily Oklahoman), I have "dutifully" written features, columns, editorials and "hard" news stories on every subject of which one can think.

According to Mark Twain (Samuel Clemens) who is one of my favorite writers, the duties of a journalist: *". . . is to keep the universe thoroughly posted con- cerning murders and street fights, balls, theaters, and park trains, and churches, and lectures, and school houses, and city military affairs, and highway robberies, and Bible Societies, and hay wagons, and a thousand other things, which it is in the province of local reporters to keep track of and magnify into undue importance for the instruction of the readers."*

— Territorial enterprise, Virginia City, Nevada Territory

Over the years I have been graciously awarded and recognized by my peers, and by the Missouri, Arkansas and Oklahoma Press Associations as well as the Associated Press. I won Arkansas' "Best Editorial" award one year; Best Newspaper and Features in Oklahoma a few times, and in 1977, from Missouri the "National Farm Writer of the Year" award which netted me an all-expense paid [Ciba-Geigy Chemical Corp.] two-week tour of Europe.

But I also have given myself to a second calling in what seems a contradiction or enigma at times — that of a bi-vocational Baptist preacher. Much as with my journalism career, preaching [the preparation and delivery of sermons] was advanced with on-the-job training although I must also claim "gifting and calling" in both vocations.

My preaching grew out of "giving my testimony" of being converted to Christ and living out my life as a Christian in the "news" business. After sensing the call to preach, I began pastoring small Baptist churches [first was country church near Malta Bend, Mo.], and when a could get some seminary training at places like Courts Redford School of

Theology in Boliver, Mo., Criswell Bible Institute and Oklahoma Baptist University. For a time I did evangelism and became an associate of the then popular "Prophecy In The News" television ministry in Oklahoma City. I have long been a student of Bible Prophecy and studied and/or preached through the Book of Revelation and Daniel numerous times. My favorite passages, however, as cited in this book, are from the Pauline epistles in the New Testament dealing with the Rapture of the Church and Revelation of Christ at His Second Coming.

I am including these things in this introduction because my publisher says it will help my credibility with you the reader as one who "knows what he is talking about." So be assured as a journalist and a serious student of the Bible, I have checked my sources. I have consumed many writings on these subjects, but when it comes to theological subjects like "the rapture" [catching away] of believers, "eternal life" and "soul" -- the source, of course, is Holy Scripture — The Bible — the revealed Word of God.

Even though I am approaching this from a Biblical or Christian World View, it is hoped that those with other views will at least read and weigh this idea of pets in the afterlife. Everyone has a world view. Some are religious with other bibles and gods. Most are secular and informed by secular education, humanist thought and philosophy. Talk to three different people out there in the hedges and highways and you will likely hear three different and opposing views of the world.

v.

There are even different and debatable ideas among those who call themselves Christians, and yes even among those that would be identified as orthodox or fundamental — especially when it comes to subjects like "the rapture" and "the millennium" two of the heavies dealt with in this treatise on "Lost Paradise, Found" — a new heaven and a new earth populated by people (and animals).

So here we go. Whether you believe or don't believe -- if you have ever wondered about what happens after this life, or about any kind of continuum if today there was a concluding event; if you are a dog lover; a student of eschatology; a curious seeker; or a died-in-the wool, can't help yourself skeptic — this book is offered.

🐾 🐾 🐾

. . . in brief, this book is about

Hounds, Heaven and the Hereafter

If you have a dog, cat or other pet — say a beagle (a class of their own), and ever think about heaven and life after death this book is for you. It is about "hounds, heaven and the hereafter." Even if you do not accept all of the author's dogma (pardon the pun), if you are an animal lover and ever wonder what your pet is thinking (or imagine what they would say to you if they could talk back in a human voice) you will identify with this book.

The author takes plenty of liberty in presenting his beagle's persona — extra fanciful at times — but stays with proof verses on matters of scriptural claims regarding subjects of beginnings, the fall of man, salvation and redemption . . . and eschatology [the part of theology concerned with death, judgment, and the final destiny of the soul and of humankind . . . and in this case, animal kind or the animal kingdom.]

But besides presenting the case for an on-going human-animal relationship beyond this life, the book which may come across for some as a Bible study, looks at real life issues albeit sometimes from the viewpoint of a dog with human like perception.

This is a book about a lot of things — but more than anything else it is a book about a Pilgrim, a "born again" believer in Christ who happens to be a dog lover (me), believing that he and his dog (a beagle or beagle-mix named "Sadie") could spend eternity together in a place called Heaven.

In the mean time — waiting and watching — Sadie Sue Dog and Loving Master Don are nearly inseparable. When there is necessary part- ing, both are accused of suffering "separation anxiety disorder" (SAD). They don't know if they like that word "disorder" but there is admission that the two are "happiest" spending time together — playing, riding, fish- ing, hunting, boating — and talking about the issues of life and life here- after.

There is seldom disagreement over such things as politics, religion or food choices.

Most of the time Sadie Dog is chasing rabbits and treeing squirrels, digging up moles or just digging. There is some disharmony over the digging and Sadie's inner clock. There are holes all over the yard, and an hour before the sun comes up Sadie is sure that's when Master Don is supposed to be up. At that time [and at least one other time during the night] Sadie comes barking. Count on it, at about 2:30 a.m. she wants out — to check the yard and take care of business, making sure some varmint hasn't taken over her territory. The day begins about 5:30. Beyond that, the routine is ever-changing.

What follows here is the sharing of life's challenges . . . and conversations between the author and his dog about them. Sadie provides some comic relief when the topic gets too serious.

Unless otherwise noted Bible references are from the King James Version of the Holy Bible. Other references permission as granted.

Acknowledgment:

Thanks to my buddy-girl Sadie for being such a willing subject and allowing me to put words in her mouth "for the cause." Many Rib Crib bones are coming your way Sadie.

And thanks to Granny who kept reminding me of approaching deadlines with those words, "how's the Sadie book coming along?" And for her proofreading.

And to others — even you with raised eyebrows — when I told you of this project and some of my conversations with Sadie.

And of course to the Master, my Master whom I have grown so much closer to as I traversed through His Word and have interchanged with one of His creatures — a loyal companion which I have come to be- lieve is more than just merely "on loan to me for a while."

—Don Diehl, July 2015

Also dedicated to Bro. Gary Woodard who waits for us there.

CHAPTER 1

Winsome Sadie Shows Up

"Well little beagle pup," I said thinking out loud, "when I finally talked Granny into letting me have a beagle dog, which by the way, she hasn't signed off on yet, I was thinking you would be full-grown, a boy dog, very obedient and house broke.

"And I was planning to name you something like 'Bugle Boy,' 'Bullet' or 'Bagel'.

"Anyway," I said as I looked at the furry little animal snuggled in my slouch fishing hat, "I've never seen a cuter little puppy than you — bashful and a little on the lazy side when it comes to being playful. Can't you walk more than three steps before you set or fall over?

"Come on, let's go show you to Granny," I told her. "And stay winsome, now. Granny's a softie."

While I was visiting a man and his wife in West Tulsa, the phone rang. I had come to invite them to a fish fry at the church. I also knew he was a crappie fisherman and might have some extra fish in the deep freeze he would "like to donate to the cause."

The couple was not sure they could make the fish fry but wanted to give the church a good batch of frozen crappie. As we visited, and be- fore I collected the fish, the phone rang and the woman answered.

"Well," she said to the person on the line, "I think you should talk to Grandpa about it," and with that, handed the phone to the gentleman. Waiting to say thanks for the fish and farewell, I listened.

Seems the granddaughter had for some time wanted a puppy and had responded to a Craigslist advertisement about some "free purebred Beagle pups."

The man repeated the youngster's side of the conversation as though he wanted grandma to hear the wisdom he was bestowing in responding to the granddaughter's request. [Most of us grandpas stand guilty as accused when it comes to granting requests to grand- daughters. I well- knew what was going to happen].

"Yeah, I'm sure they are all cute like you. No, only one," he said. "And you will have to care for it — we're not going to babysit a beagle for you. Is it healthy? How old is it? Weaned? What, 13 puppies? No, what did I say? Only one . . . do you hear what Grandpa is saying?"

That's when I said to the woman, "Little puppies . . .? You

know, I've been thinking I would like to have a beagle myself."

The gentleman overheard.

"Hey dear," he said to his granddaughter, "hang on . . . there's a preacher here and he wants one of those puppies."

"What? Let me check," he said. "They all look alike? Tan, black and white? Well, after all, they're beagles. How many boys, girls? Hang on . . .

"You want one don't you?" he asked me. ". . . only one male not spoken for."

"Yeah, I'll take it," I said without much more thought (maybe a very, very quick prayer) and absolutely no permission from the one at home who already had weighed in on the matter. And that on the negative side of us becoming dog owners.

The pup was small enough to fit into the fishing hat. I didn't have a cage when the little girl handed me one of two little beagle puppies she had brought to her grandparents' home in West Tulsa. The eleven-year- old, thinking perhaps she had manipulated the situation and that grandpa was going to allow two pups, had already named the weary little thing with sad eyes — "Saddee."

"Sadie it is," I said, making a quick spelling and sound change as if I did not understand exactly. I admired her efforts at purpose- ly nam- ing the puppy as if she was going to have two sister beagles, but I didn't want to tag my pet with such a "sad" name. I did not raise the issue about the male beagle I thought I was going to be getting. Neither the little girl or Sadie's sister pup would ever see their 'Saddee' again. Eh, or perhaps they will some day in a special way.

Stay tuned.

Puppy Sadie and our granddaughter Harmony Grace

CHAPTER 2

Starting the Conversation

When we pulled away from that West Tulsa residence it hit me. Sadie was not home free yet. And I may have entered one of those cove- nants I wasn't sure I could keep. Yet I could tell that Sadie was willing to keep her end of the bargain — whatever that bargain was.

It would not be long before it became apparent that this was not just a matter of getting a new family pet. This was a rescue operation for at least two of God's insecure creatures — Sadie and myself.

There may be an instance in which what I am about to pen may not apply but I can not think of one. Every relationship begins with and is maintained by conversation. The word 'conservation' is interesting. Mainly because of our modern dictionary we make the word to mean 'talk' as in verbal communication that includes two entities — a speaker and a listener who swap roles — one speaks while the other listens, and vice versa.

In the King James English the word 'conversation' means much more than talk.* It means manner of life. Check it out the next time you are reading one of the New Testament epistles. In the letter to the Philippians for instance, the Apostle writes in 1:27: "Only let your conversation be as it becometh the gospel of Christ . . ." and in the English Standard Version: "Only let your manner of life be worthy of the gospel of Christ . . ." [Underline emphasis mine].

As I drove along Route 66 toward home I kept glancing at what was laying in the seat beside me and there and then began to do something that has since become second nature — converse with a hound dog and interpreting her response.

Can hounds talk? Of course they can. Just ask any dog owner. They talk using sound as well as silence. Sometimes they bark out the message. They whimper, whine, growl and — like humans — moan and groan. They sigh, they yawn — and contrary to what some experts tell you — they smile and frown.

They talk with their eyes, tilt of the head, perk of the ear and — big time — wag of the tale. The hair that stands up on the back of their necks, unlike humans, is actually visible. Dogs are true communicators. Who doesn't get it? A drool of the tongue and half-closed eye-lid when a human lightly scratches the ear says "I so like that." And a turned-up fully-exposed belly begs "please rub me!"

So did I then and there begin (and do I now) carry on verbal con- versations with Sadie Sue? Is there audible speech taking place? Well, I guess we (Sadie and I) will just have to leave that up to you.

"So what do you think, Sadie Sue?" I asked.

"I don't know mister . . . and is it 'mister' or 'master'? Right now, I am just trying to figure out what my name is and if you are talking to me," Sadie answered.

"'Think, you ask," Sadie continues. "You do my talking for me, master, I'll do the thinking."

And with that I hear Sadie thinking.

Actually wondering about a lot of things:

"Where are we going? What's next? All this movement has me scared to death," she said. "See me shaking here?

"What's that wet, stinking stuff they rubbed all over my fur? Got my skin crawling for sure.

"And where are all those other little creatures with hair like mine I have been dealing with since my eyes first opened? Where is Mama Dog and her belly's comfort and warmth? I am just learning about dog food, yuk, and you want me to understand and speak English?"

"Tall order, huh, Sadie Sue?"

"Sure is mister master, whatever. You keep on talking, I have to dose. You talk about things way too deep for me and I'll just go to sleep." "Well, I know something about that," I said to Sadie. "I preach some you know . . . sermonize? Anyway, I'm used to folks dosing off while I'm talking. You know Sadie, I don't think I have ever preached to a dog before.

"Sadie are you listening? Sadie Sue . . ."

Well that's about the way I spent the first hour or so with my new beagle pup. I indeed understood as we rode along together that there was a crossroads kind of thing taking place in the journey of a man with more mortal years behind him than before him — and in the life of a dog — a pup just beginning.

---

*ORIGIN: Middle English (in the sense 'living among, familiarity, intimacy'): via Old French from Latin conversatio(n-), from the verb *conversari*

ABOUT CONVERSATION

It really is true. Relationships begin with and are maintained by conversation. We already have talked about conversation being more than talk — it's also walk, or "manner of life" (lifestyle). Conversation is what seals our covenant — yea, keeps our promises and commitments. As a process it is a "bonding" — or that which joins two people or entities, i.e. a man and his dog.

In a sense we can say even the Creator with his creation began with conversation. "In the beginning," it says in Genesis 1:1, "God created the heavens and the earth."

"The first verse of the Bible gives us a satisfying and useful account of the origin of the earth and the heavens," writes commentator Matthew Henry. "The faith of humble Christians understands this better than the fancy of the most learned men. From what we see of heaven and earth, we learn the power of the great Creator."

Psalm 33:9 says, "For he spake, and it was done; he commanded, and it stood fast.

In John 1 ' "In the beginning was the Word, and the Word was with God, and the Word was God". The phrase "the Word" (a translation of the Greek word 'Logos.') refers to Jesus. Or as we refer to Him "the incarnate word."

"And the Word was made flesh, and dwelt among us, (and we beheld his glory, the glory as of the only begotten of the Father,) full of grace and truth." — John 1:14.

Then in John, Chapter 4, we have that Word in 'conversation' with the Samaritan Woman as — Jesus the soul winner — on a very personal level leading one to himself.

The BeeGees may not be a Gospel music group but the song "Words" could sure be a Gospel song in that regard: "This world has lost it's glory, lets start a brand new story now, my love. Right now . . . It's only words, and words are all I have, to take Your heart away."

Words — thought, spoken and lived out — are powerful. Call it friendship, fellowship or relationship. We dog lovers talk to our dogs and our dogs talk to us. It may be a divine thing.

CHAPTER 3

Beagle, Meet the Boss

There used to be a man in our town — a Harley rider who had a small dog — terrier [Jack Russell type] — that became a fixture on his bike. Any time you saw the man riding, you would see the dog perched there and marvel at how it could so stay in place and with immense delight. That kind of companion idea came to me several times when I was out fishing and took note of lone fishermen with their dog aboard their boat.

One day I pointed out to my wife Janell — most of the time my reluctant fishing buddy — "that's what I need, a canine fishing buddy."

"Prob-ab-ly," she returned. Pronounced that way the word is one of her favorite negotiation terms. It means yeah, but not [zilch, nada] likely to happen. Since I was retiring from daily-deadlined newspapers (which would give me nightmares for years to come) I had contemplated many things to occupy my time.

I scarcely would have time to care for a dog, Janell would argue "Besides, what would you do with a dog when you just wanted to take off for a few days?" she asked. "Who's going to care for it when we're gone . . . feed and water?

"Have you thought about those things? I think not," she said.

I was replaying those lines in my head as I turned off Route 66 and traversed the final few blocks to the house.

It was about then that I began questioning myself. Is this another case of not first getting permission then later asking for forgiveness? Surely, a beagle hound is not a high maintenance animal. But what do I know. I didn't even Google to learn anything about the Beagle breed. All I know is that they are supposed to be good rabbit hunters. And I have always liked that feverish high pitch bay for which they are famous. Hmmm, I haven't heard this one do that yet. Wonder if she will bark a lot at night?

Hey, wait a minute. I have been praying haven't I? I've been asking for God's blessings and that His will be done in my life. My life's verse is Matthew 6:33 "Seek ye first the kingdom of God and all these things shall be added unto you." Psalm 37:4 says, "Delight thyself also in the LORD; and he shall give you the desires of your heart."

Get ye behind me Satan. I'm feeling OK with this. Besides, I already know Janell is a pushover when it comes to babies of any kind — kittens, pups, chicks and humans. And look how cute and fuzzy this beagle pup is there all cuddled up that way.

We pull into the driveway.

"Well Sadie, you ready to meet the boss?" I ask.

She opens and moves her eyes upward. Head still down.

I carefully collect the whole bundle, hat and all, and walk to the back screen door cradling the package on my forearm and elbow ready to "surprise" my wife.

"What is that?" she asks, meeting me halfway in the opened

door. She was expecting packages of frozen fish.

"Look at this little thing," I said. "This is Sadie Sue. She's a beagle pup."

"Whose?" Janell asked.

"Ours . . . mine," I said. "I told them we would take one. There was a whole litter, thirteen in all. She really needs us."

"Oh no you don't. Don, we're not doing this," Janell protests. "I thought we said we were not going to have any more pets. Them who? You need to take her right back. You're not bringing her in here. You will have to fix her a pen outside."

"Prob-ab-ly," I said.

By the time I told the story (with a rescue slant of course), Janell had the little girl pup out of the hat and towel and was tickling her beneath the chin. Sadie walked about three steps and plopped down in a crawl, nearly a layover position.

Just then I could see it plainly. Looking up at Granny and making eye contact through those "sad" appealing eyes, I knew what had just happened. Sadie pulled it off without even trying. Granny melted.

The questions now were about food and water, house-breaking and a cage, sleeping patterns, shots and "what are those little black things in her fur?"

"I think they are dead fleas," I said. "The little girl's mom gave the pups a bath and dipped them for fleas and ticks."

Sadie, however, was still loaded with seed ticks — live ones as we would learn the next day at the veterinarian's office. We also would soon learn the costs associated with tick and flea control, with "shots" [vaccines], medicines and preventive medicines, about heart worms and grooming. And spaying.

As it turned out, Sadie was indeed a rescue operation. She had been badly infested with parasites and was malnourished. It wasn't (although it seemed) her nature to walk three steps and fall over. That is just all she could muster. She was not really in very good health — but a fighter we could tell.

It would be at least a week or two before she began chewing up everything she could get her jaws close to — fiddle stands, shoes, belts, books and otherwise indestructible plastic toys. By the time she was a month old she could nearly devour a tennis ball and eat the whole cover of a children's book. She would swallow the hands and feet of little plastic animals that made for colorful poop. Did I say she loved to chew? That phase would only be superseded by her current one — digging.

Good news (and we have learned more by doing than by Googling), Beagles are stubborn but very trainable. They love approval more than treats, and really want to please their humans. At any rate, the little fuzzy was not long about working her way into the hearts of Granny and Peep. "Pepe" (one syllable) is what the grand- kids call me. Sadie and I decided early on she would be addressing me during periods of great conversation as "Loving Master."

We have now lived through our second Fourth of July together — Sadie, Granny and I. Still at times, Sadie's expressions are much as they were that night we met up two years ago.

Sadie doesn't like fireworks — their sounds, mainly. I'm not sure how she will do if we ever go hunting and I actually fire a gun. She sought refuge in my office room the other night when all the fireworks were exploding. I recalled the security she found in that old slouch hat when I first brought her home. Today, that hat along with caps, socks and house shoes still serve as security blankets. I think, kind of hope, Sadie always will remain a pup.

As stated earlier, Granny (first Jannie Granny, then shortened to just Granny) my wife of 25 years had shunned suggestions for some time that we should get a dog. We had befriended cats before. (I don't think you ever own a cat, you can only befriend them. Perhaps we never really "own" any animals. "God owns the cattle [animals] on a thousand hills," the Scripture says. Our dominion over them is more of a supreme stewardship assigned by God himself.)

There was first "Starving Stray" who gave us a litter of kittens which gave us even more kittens and a very necessary education about the importance of spaying and neutering. Her name had been changed to "Grandma Cat" before we got the practice fully implemented. Some daughters, granddaughters and grandsons along with always a new crop of strays ensured we were cat-attached. We had cats around the house as long as they could survive the cars, diseases, poisons and each other.

There was "Nubby," very special and a survivor of a mama cat who was trying to cull him from her litter; "White Tiger," a deaf tomcat. (Did you know white cats with blue eyes are often deaf?); "Mr. Sleepy Eyes," "Butterscotch" and "Blackie." Butterscotch survived a car attack but later had to be put to sleep — in my arms. I cried — quite a bit — and buried her in our private pet cemetery. I think Blackie missed her too. He soon just went away. Birds started returning to the yard and we didn't have to impose on the neighbors to put out feed and water for the cats when we were going to be gone. Our cats were in and out. They liked it out.

You don't fence or herd cats. There's other difference between cats and dogs — understated. And what about cats in Heaven? Nine lives or everlasting life? Well, as we might say in dog terms, let's stay on point. The question we plan to answer is what happens to our pets at the consumption of the ages.

CHAPTER 4

Regal Beagles Go Way Back

Something else we learned at that first vet visit, and I'm still not sure I am settled it as so. Sadie may not be a purebred Beagle. OMG (and let that stand for Oh My Gracious). She has the right colors — black, tan and white, but her hair is a little too long, she now stands a little taller than most Beagles and weighs slightly more than the 30- pound range.

"But this I can say, Sadie," I tell her. "It really doesn't make a bit of difference. I am calling you my Beagle and because of that connection, not your breeding, you are one heaven-bound hound."

"There's a life lesson here Sadie," I tell her. "And I will have several of these for you so pay attention. It is true for humans and I suspect for canines like yourself.

"There are four things humans want. It is the way God wired us. And it is in seeking those four things that can get us all mixed up.

"What are those four things Loving Master?" Sadie wonders.

"Well, I'm so glad you asked, Sadie Sue. I believe you will readily understand these," I said.

"The four things wanted and needed in life are: One, to be loved; Two, to win approval; Three, to be part of something (a cause or a group, eh, a pack); and Four, to make an impact (leave a legacy, be remembered).

"What is interesting (and it takes a lifetime for some of us to figure it out) is that all four of those things are completely fulfilled in a personal relationship with a king — King Jesus. He completely and unconditionally loves, accepts, joins himself to His creation and makes life count for all eternity.

"You see, Sadie," I explain. "There is a kingdom of man, there is the animal kingdom, there is an insect kingdom, there is a plant kingdom and a mineral kingdom.

"Are you with me Sadie? Did you dose off?"

"I'm right here Loving Master, but I must admit, you lost me there a couple of times. Do those things have anything to do with beagles — being a dog? And how does that personal relationship thing apply to me?

"Now that love and acceptance thing I get," Sadie says.

"I live to love and be loved. And I really like it when you say '"Good girl, Sadie."' I like being a part of all that goes on around here. I really like it when we get in the truck and go to the park and places. I know we are making memories. I guess that is why you and Granny are always taking those pictures."

"You're right, Sadie," I say. "I feel like we are having a good , deep conversation here — maybe even a little intellectual.

"Humans and dogs are not the same. We're wired very differ-ent," I tell Sadie. "Humans act out of something we call free will. Members of the animal kingdom (that would be you) act out of in-stinct. Your free will as an animal is informed by your instinct. I don't think humans have instinct, only a conscience . . . and intellect.

"Anyway, we will talk more about that when we discuss sin, salvation and grace — and beagles in eternity!

"What I am trying to get to here, Sadie, is a life lesson on measuring up. As with humans, so it is I suppose with dogs. There always will be those who have an ideal mold or class for you to fit into; a criteria for you to meet in order to be the perfect beagle — or to be a beagle at all. They say your fur has to be a certain color, your hair a certain length or no length at all. They say you have to walk a certain way and bark and bay like a beagle . . . and chase rabbits."

Then I tell Sadie, "If you are a beagle mix, that's OK. (Better than being a mixed-up beagle). And, bottom line, you are loved just the way you are."

I really like some of those dog jokes: This little boy was walking through the market place with his doggie. A man happened to ask the lad, "what kind of mutt do you have there son?"

"Why, he's a police dog," answered the boy.

It was plain to see the man had rightly identified the dog as a mongrel. [mongrel: a long-haired mutt of doubtful pedigree.]

"Well," said the man, "he don't look much like a police dog to me." To that without hesitation, the little boy said: "Well he's in the secret service. He's an undercover police dog, don't you know?"

The beagle is an interesting breed

Now, I'm not claiming there were actual beagles on Noah's Ark, but there were two dogs — one male and one female — from which the beagle came. I have done some research and learned that today's modern beagle dates to the middle ages and probably comes from a group of Southern Hounds in England bred to be harriers (hunters of hares). There are hundreds of breeds of dogs — 150 in America according to the American Kennel Club — hundreds more across the world.

Beagles rank about number 4 on the list of the top 25 breeds .

There have been a lot of new breeds since the landing of the ark, but if you wonder what the dogs on the ark were like, check out the Asian Wolf. Experts tell us it is the truest ancestor to modern dog. Of course remember, much of the information passed on to us today is akin to National Geo- graphic supposition.

Always apply your biblical worldview of knowledge and truth. When they suppose that dogs were probably the first "domesticated" animal you can hit the "wait-a-minute" button. We know biblically that dogs as other animals all were "domestic" in the original creation — in the Garden before the fall of man. [Remember, there was no dying, disease, killing, shedding of blood before the fall. Animals were meant for companions in creation, not for food and clothing]. These become important points as we consider a restored creation — Paradise lost and Paradise found.

Man is egocentric to the core. Adam and Eve had pets in their home, did they not? When the first man and woman were driven from the Garden, the animals had to go too. And when God gave instructions for the building of the ark to endure the flood judgement it was not just for the saving of eight humans.

So what of this Regal Beagle?
Royalty, if you will?

While I was writing the first edition of this book, a preacher friend of mine passed. [We don't use the word "died" when one of the faith passes. That's a carryover from my journalistic career. Believers, as we should, say "went home to be with the Lord."] At rest with the King. *"Absent from the body, present with the Lord."* — II Corinthians 5:8

Brother Gary and his wife, Susan, were fascinated with our royal beagle "Sadie" and with the prospect of a book defending the proposition of pets being with us in Heaven. I used to worry Susan when I encouraged Gary to get himself a beagle. Finally, Janell and I got him one — a wind-up model that jumped around and barked just like the real issue. They named the toy "Rapture."

The estimation of Sadie the beagle grew even more around the church when the pastor heard that a beagle (who looks a lot like Sadie) — yes, a beagle — won the Westminster Best in Show honors at Madison Square Garden [February 2015].

The "Regal Beagle" [some reporter's creation, not mine] was a 15-inch, 4-year-old named Miss P. And get this, she beat out a Shih Tzu owned by newspaper heiress Patty Hearst [yes, that one] and a Portuguese water dog — a cousin of the Obamas' family pet, "Sunny." The writer went on to report "Matisse, the Portie, was an early favorite but came up short. Hearst's pooch, Rocket, won in the toy category, but couldn't compete with Miss P."

PHOTO BY STEVE SURFMAN (USED BY PERMISSION OF WESTMINSTER KENNEL CLUB).
"Miss P," the beagle that won the Best of Show at 2015 Westminster Dog Show in Madison Square Garden in February. Handler was Will Alexander.

Someone has said dogs don't laugh. I believe they do and cry too, I think. Sadie and I had us a good chuckle when I told her about Miss P. And we also grieved at Pastor Gary's passing.

"We'll see him again won't we master?" Sadie asked.

Her thoughts were again on the passing of the man who actually left a hand-written note to her one day attached to a big cookie. It was in the shape of a milk bone. The note said, "For Sadie." The treat had been left on the pew in the foyer of the church building. Gary had anticipated a visit from the two of us. He had Susan bring one of the treats that she had found at a bakery "just for Sadie."

"See him again? Yes, I believe we will Sadie. Maybe sooner than we think. And he will be glad to see you again too."

"Tell me about the Rapture, Loving Master," Sadie said.

"You mean that toy beagle that was on the table for a time before we gave it to the preacher . . . the one you wanted to chew up?"

"No, about the Heavenly trip you keep talking about," she said.

"And I wasn't going to chew it up. I just wanted to play with it."

The Beagle by common definition is a breed of small to medium-sized hound dog. It is similar in appearance to the foxhound but smaller with shorter legs and has somewhat longer ears. The scent hounds were primarily developed for tracking rabbit and small game and sometimes deer. Their great sense of smell and tracking instinct also makes them good detection dogs for prohibited agricultural imports and foodstuffs. Beagles are intelligent but single-minded. They are popular pets because of their size, even tempered and lack of inherited health problems.

Growing up . . . looking up . . . going up!

CHAPTER 5

So Do Dogs Go to Heaven?

When I called Westminster Kennel Club to obtain permission to publish a photo of "Miss P," I talked to publicity director David Frei. He also is the author of "Angel On A Leash," a heartwarming collection of stories about therapy dogs and the people they serve. The book defines the "ministry" that Frei shares with his wife, Chaplain Cheri- lyn Frei. She is director of spiritual care at the Ronald McDonald House of New York. David is known as "the Voice of Westminster," the famous New York kennel club for which he has worked for the past two decades. We talked about dogs and our books.

"Yes, she will," he said with certainty when I told him the title of my book, 'Will My Beagle Go With Me In The Rapture?'

Then he shared a verse of scripture he uses when asked questions of dogs in the hereafter. Job 12:10 says of God: "In whose hand is the soul of every living thing, and the breath of all mankind."

Some time ago, not long after I brought Sadie home from Wes-

Tulsa, got her doctored up at the vets — shots, spayed and ridded of fleas and ticks — we started doing a lot of fishing. Well, I was doing the fishing, Sadie was watching . . . and listening. You understand that "fishing" is not just fishing?

No offense to my long-time fishing buddy, Jake. He and I used to hit the area lakes and the Verdigris River each spring to gather in some of the best "slab" crappie one could find. Jake would catch two to my one nearly every time. I could write a book about some of our experiences. Jake is older now. So am I. We find weather, water conditions and life itself has to be just right before we venture out in the boat fishing.

Jake, a Euchi Indian also is a Pentecostal preacher. I'm a Baptist. We were more even on politics than church doctrine but shared a lot of life's values along with a supreme taste for fresh crappie.

Likewise, no offense to my wife, Janell (Jannie or Granny). She's a pretty good "buddy" to fish with as well but seldom has a pole in the water.

"But Sadie Sue," as I told her on a recent fishing trip, "you are the best fishing buddy ever. I wasn't so sure to start with, but you have grown to love the bass boat almost as much as the pick-em up truck."

"Well indeed I have master," she responded, "as long as there's a breeze out here and when you're moving the boat along at a good enough clip that my ears stand out as I position myself there on the bow like a lookout."

"And I like the way you talk," Sadie continues. "I mean, would you use words like pick-em up truck if you were talking to another human?"

"Good point, Sadie," I say.

That's usually the case when the two of us talk religion or politics. Sadie may not always agree, but she appears to be grinning as if she does. She also seems to provide that comic relief needed any time politics or religion are discussed.

There has been a time or two we had problems when we've been fishing. Once when Granny was with us she advocated the wearing of a life jacket by Sadie.

"I kept telling her you could swim," didn't I Sadie? "Though I admit I had not seen you do so."

I insisted that dogs just know how to swim. You don't have to teach them like you do humans. Dogs do it instinctively. [I wrote earlier about that major difference between humans and animals].

"God has wired dogs that way," I told Granny.

Then it happened. Point proven. I was trying to land a nice bass and Sadie thought it good to share the excitement and got a little too close to my elbow and angling skills. Trying to make sure I had the hook set, I elbowed Sadie right into the lake.

Sadie may have been wired to know how to swim but she still seemed frightened. And Granny really got excited.

There have been times since when Sadie had a need to exit the boat to swim to shore or be pulled from the water back into the boat.

"I love you and trust you, master," she told me after a couple of those mishaps and recounting the adventures. "But I have to say I'm not so sure that you did not push me into the water on purpose at least one of those times."

"Well maybe that one time," I admitted to Sadie, "after you had rolled around on that smelly carcass at the shoreline right before we got in the boat. You smelled awful. I couldn't even concentrate on fishing."

I remember after that and subsequent experiences trying to fig ure out why Sadie and other dogs like to roll in things that are, well just nasty. Fish remains are among the worst only equaled by goose poop. Then there are the piles of fresh cow or horse manure, green deer poop in the woods or a dead animal carcass. Disgusting. I keep thinking Sadie will remember my intolerance and the consequences of such actions. But like her digging, she can't seem to help herself.

In this it seems, dog nature is like human nature. Why do we roll around in nasty stuff? Especially when we know the consequences.

Maybe your beagle likes water. Mine don't. "Water's only for drinking," Sadie says. Oh she will scamper along the two or three inches of it along the sandy shore, or wade out a little further if she's trying to retrieve some slime, but Sadie doesn't voluntarily go into the depths. Nor does she like water hosed or dumped onto her.

One day after dragging Sadie from a duck poop waste site back to the camping spot to hose her down I kept telling her how bad she smelled and asking why she would roll in such stinking stuff especial- ly knowing what was sure to follow?

Now I know most of my readers don't believe Sadie Sue actually talks to me, so I know there's going to be raised eye brows if I tell you she quotes scripture. Still, as I had raised the question and Sadie's eyes made contact with mine, it came to me from Romans 7: "For the good that I would I do not: but the evil which I would not, that I do. Now if I do that which I would not, it is no more I that do it, but sin [nature] that dwells in me. I find then a law, that, when I would do good, evil is present with me."

How in Heaven's name do you respond to that?

In my Google searches I have found some acceptable theories

as to why dogs like to roll in what to human nostrils is foul-smelling and disgusting. One reason, according to some of the experts, is that the practice serves as a natural deterrent to parasites. That makes sense. I know if I was a flea or tick I wouldn't come close. Another theory is that by transferring the odor from the ground to the dog's coat, it hides her scent from other animals in the area she may be hunting. Then there is this one. Perfume. She likes the way it makes her smell to herself and to other dogs. That almost sounds too human, but we have to remember, dogs do not greet each other with handshakes and hugs — it's with the smeller.

"It is only that one time I pushed you overboard," I answer Sadie. "But I also remember that one time you misjudged the distance between the boat and the dock? You came up short by a couple of feet and went into the deep at the edge of the dock."

"Yes, and that was scary, master," Sadie recalled. "Very scary."

"Well, I reached down quickly and snatched you right out of that dangerous situation. Saved you! I will never forget the look in your eyes when I brought you back into the boat," I told her.

"Thank you master. I love you," she said. "And I could tell how much you loved me that day too!"

"OK, so Sadie let's talk about the rapture. That snatching you out of the water into the boat is a perfect illustration. There is coming a day when the Master of all will snatch (or catch away) His children from this earth and take them to Heaven.

"Maybe before we single out the rapture, we should talk about Heaven. We can't understand the rapture apart from understanding something of Heaven.

"I know you do not concern yourself with such matters, Sadie And being a dog, you are not accountable to do so, but because of the way things are in the world and because I am getting older, suppose, I have really been giving this a lot of thought.

"Are you listening, Sadie?" I ask semi-seriously.

Sadie is at least watching me watch her. Her mouth is opened slightly, her tongue drooping barely beyond her teeth. To me it seems she is smiling. Her eyes blink slowly. (Sometimes I swear, she winks with one eye.) She pauses, gulps slightly, takes a swipe at her nose with her tongue and returns to the smily-looking pant."

"Yes, I'm listening Loving Master," she seems to say.

"OK, Sadie, I know that you like to go with me wherever I go. And I like that too. So I was wondering, Sadie, if I should sort of explain to you about Heaven — since it's a place where we will spend eternity — if you will understand?"

I believe the earthly blessings that so delight us here are just a foretaste of what awaits us in glory. The notion of being with loved ones including our pets in a place called Heaven after this journey on earth ends is more than contemplative. It is reasonable . . . and I believe has a scriptural basis.

Sadie and I were at the park near our house the other morning. We go there nearly every day. It is close by, but we still take the truck. If there aren't any other walkers near, I just carry the leash un- attached. It allows both of us some freedom.

Sadie chases and trees squirrel and digs for moles. After a full trip around the park's walking trail I begin to coax Sadie back to the pick-up. I get in and tap the horn. She immediately begins to dig frantically as if she has but a few seconds to get one more hole dug. The park people love us, I'm sure. I try to take a rake with me some- times, or kick dirt back into the holes.

As I pull around the circle, Sadie hurries to the fence of a nearby neighbor to arouse Ferdo and Fido (not their real names I'm sure), a couple of medium sized mutts who from their side of the fence chase Sadie up and down its distance six to eight times, barking and raising Cain. Sadie already thinks she's in Heaven. All this running, frolicking, and chasing with the master nearby.

"So Sadie Sue," I ask, "do you want to go to heaven?"

"I don't know, Loving Master," she answers. "I'm just learning what the park is about. I kind of like this park. Do they have squirrels like this in Heaven?" (Some of that comic relief).

"Good night, Sadie," I respond to the prospect. "I have been reading, and studying the plausibility of pets going to heaven and dogs having souls and . . . well, you bring up the question of tree-dwelling rodents being in Heaven."

"Well you asked me if I wanted to go to Heaven and I just wanted to know what it's going to be like," Sadie apologizes. "What's going to be there? Trees, grass, ground to dig in, smells for my nose? You know about my beagle nose don't you master? Are there going to be squirrels?"

"Short answer, Sadie — yes," I offer. "And, un-huh, I sure know or at least am learning about that nose. But let's not get ahead of ourselves. By the way, I'm surprised you didn't ask about rabbits. After all, you're supposed to be a rabbit dog."

"Yeah, are there going to be rabbits in Heaven?" Sadie taunts.

"Well, Sadie Dog, I can see this is going to be tougher than I thought. Not only am I going to have to defend canine immortality here, I'm going to have to deal with squirrel and rabbit?"

"It's OK Master. I'm just chewing your leg. None of those things really matter to me. If you, Loving Master, are going to be in Heaven, then Heaven is where I want to be."

"Now, Sadie. That is so sweet. And I'm thinking, that is also a great attitude for Christians to have about 'The Master' as they study and contemplate all of the things and beauty of Heaven."

Sadie praying?

CHAPTER 6

The Mystery of the Church

Who is waiting for you over there?

My mother went home to Heaven years ago. My father died [or more correct in the believer's vernacular, went to sleep in Jesus] when I was a junior in high school.

I believe my parents, my grandmother, a half-brother as well as many other believers in Jesus Christ whom I have known over the years, including those whose farewells I have officiated over from pulpits across the way are in Heaven. But every time I hear that old "Johnny and June" song "Far Side Banks of Jordan" it is my mother I visualize "sitting drawing pictures in the sand" and when she sees me coming, rising up with a shout "And comes running through the shallow water reaching for my hand."

It's a wonderful song. However, as I have studied the portrayal, I realize it could only play out that way if I pass before the rapture occurs. In which case, the reunion will actually then take place in the air. Those in Heaven now are there in spiritual bodies. The physical body is in the grave — dust or ashes — maybe buried in a cemetery, at sea or just scattered. God knows where every DNA carrying particle resides. When the rapture and first resurrection occurs, the heavenly residents will come with Jesus. Their bodies will be fashioned together and resurrected from the earth to be reunited with their spiritual ones in the air — glorified. And we which are alive will be [caught away] raptured and meet them in the air.

Paul reveals (or unveils) the mystery of the church and its ultimate position as a bride presented to the coming bridegroom (Christ). " . . . that he might present the church to himself in splendor, without spot or wrinkle or any such thing, that she might be holy and without blemish," it reads in Ephesians 5:25-27, ESV.

The Apostle writes in the New Testament "Behold, I shew you a mystery; We shall not all sleep, but we shall all be changed, In a moment, in the twinkling of an eye, at the last trump: for the trumpet shall sound, and the dead shall be raised incorruptible, and we shall be changed." —1 Corinthians 15:51-52.

Remember when we say "sleep" we're talking about the physical body not the soul. A great truth to grasp is that the soul is eternal and that one day "this corruptible must put on incorruption, and this mortal must put on immortality. So when this corruptible shall have put on incorruption, and this mortal shall have put on immortality, then shall be brought to pass the saying that is written, Death is swallowed up in victory." These are concluding verses from the Apostle's first letter to the Corinthians, chapter 15. Reading that chapter in conjunction with what is said here will prove beneficial.

FOUR PINNACLE TRUTHS

There are four great truths that have been like pinnacles for me in my Christian walk. Yea, liberating. The Bible, God's infallible Word, contains principles, prophesies and promises. There are definitely more than four great truths, but these four that I mention for me have become like pit stops in the race of life that I can pull into and be refueled, refurbished and readied for the next lap of the race.

I am not going to list them in any kind of order here or elaborate fully (that would take several chapters, probably a book or two) but here they are briefly. This brief study also provides a basis for what we conclude in answering the question: "Will My Beagle Go With Me In The Rapture" and why I believe our pets will be with us in Heaven. Important: all four of these pertain primarily to believers:

No. 1. Church is not a place, Heaven is;

No. 2. Believers only die once [clue, during this life, not primarily at life's close in physical death];

No. 3. You do not have to sin; and

No. 4. Grace-provided eternity is most important thing of all

Now I am going to touch on all of these and try to explain why they have been so liberating to me personally; and encourage you to claim these truths as well. Jesus said, "I am the way, the truth and the life: no man cometh unto the Father, but by me." — John 14:6

It is interesting to note that man, it seems [apart from Lucifer and other fallen angels] is the only one of God's creatures that can be convinced there is a way to reach the Father's house other than through the redemptive blood of His son — Jesus Christ.

In John 8:32 Jesus says believers "shall know the truth, and the truth shall make you free."

Truth No. 1: When I say "Church is not a place, Heaven is," I know the statement runs counter to what we have lodged in our minds. We have been instructed to "go to church" and to "worship at the church of your choice." We have "worship centers" and "fellow- ship halls" and "sanctuaries." We even call the "church building" the "House of God" and make it sound like a home with separate rooms for different functions.

The cliches are plentiful but are often more akin to paganism than to Biblical Christianity. The Bible defines "the church" as a "body of believers in the Lord Jesus" not a brick or wood framed building on the corner of First Street and Main. If we're not careful we make "church" sound like a club, a lodge or a building complex — yea, even a religious temple.

A good Bible study on this matter is found in the conversation [John, Chapter 4] between Jesus and the Samaritan woman. You will remember her protest: "Our ancestors worshiped on this mountain, but you Jews claim that the place where we must worship is in Jerusalem."

"Woman," Jesus replied, "believe me, a time is coming when you will worship the Father neither on this mountain nor in Jerusalem. You Samaritans worship what you do not know; we worship what we do know, for salvation is from the Jews. Yet a time is coming and has now come when the true worshipers will worship the Father in the Spirit and in truth, for they are the kind of worshipers the Father seeks. God is spirit, and his worshipers must worship in the Spirit and in truth." [Vss.20-24].

So church is not a place — a temple, a synagogue, a shrine or an arbor in the mountains. Church is that group (body) of people of God known as Christians.

"All I know, master," said Sadie when I tried to explain this to her, "is that when you and Granny go to church, I get to stay home . . . or sometimes go with you and just hang out in the pickup while you're in the church."

"See what I mean, Sadie? We've even passed the language on to you," I said. "We don't 'go to church.' And 'in the church' doesn't mean being under a roof of a building even though that may be a good place to sing together, to study God's Word together, to pray together, to get better equipped for ministry — even to exercise our spiritual gifts and to fellowship [have communion] and fulfill the ordinances, i.e. Believers' Baptism and the Lord's Supper."

"Do I need to . . ." Sadie interrupts.

"Hang on there a minute, Sadie. Was you going to ask if dogs need to be baptized? Or did that word 'supper' catch your attention? I'm glad I didn't list foot-washing," I joked. "We do practice foot-washing don't we — when you come in the house after a dig."

"For all creation is waiting eagerly for that future day when God will reveal who his children really are. Against its will, all creation was subjected to God's curse. But with eager hope, the creation looks forward to the day when it will join God's children in glorious freedom from death and decay. For we know that all creation has been groaning as in the pains of childbirth right up to the present time. And we believers also groan, even though we have the Holy Spirit within us as a foretaste of future glory, for we long for our bodies to be released from sin and suffering. We, too, wait with eager hope for the day when God will give us our full rights as his adopted children, including the new bodies he has promised us." Romans 8:19-23 NLT

"And maybe we took care of that baptism thing the day you missed the dock jumping from the boat," I said jokingly.

Actually, that event is a good illustration of salvation. Sadie tried to jump onto the dock but fell short. She was in danger of destruction, but her master reached down and saved her. Lifted her up and placed her on the solid dock.'

"No, dogs do not need to be baptized. And no, you don't need to "attend church" with us Sadie. I will explain how you fit into all of this. Be patient" [a very hard thing for Sadie].

As for "church," the Bible says that Jesus loved the church and gave himself for it. [Ephesians 5:25]. Why? "That he might sanctify and cleanse it with the washing of water by the word, That he might present it to himself a glorious church, not having spot, or wrinkle, or any such thing; but that it should be holy and without blemish. [26-27].

In the Book of Revelation, chapter 19, we have, "Let us be glad and rejoice, and give honour to him: for the marriage of the Lamb is come" and in Revelation 21 the language "Come hither, I will shew thee the bride, the Lamb's wife."

It is the church that Jesus is coming for at the end of the [church] age. It is the church that's going to be raptured and resurrected. It is the church that is going to be presented to Christ at the Marriage Supper of the Lamb. Believers make up the bride, who following "the marriage supper of the Lamb" returns with Christ to "rule and reign" and ultimately forever secure the answer to the model prayer Jesus teaches us to pray "thy kingdom come, thy will be done on earth as it is in Heaven."

That phrase "thy kingdom come, thy will be done" is the where and when of God's perfect plan for creation under the rule and reign of King Jesus — the future Kingdom Age and beyond of which the Apostle writes in the eighth chapter of the Book of Romans.

We will look closer at that deeper in this book but when we talk about the church we are talking about people who "must be born again" to get into the kingdom.

Because of first man's sin, sin passed on to all of his offspring. "All have sinned and come short of the glory of God," the Bible says. In John, Chapter 3, we read about "a man of the Pharisees, named Nicodemus who came to Jesus by night with a question about the kingdom."Except a man be born again, he cannot see the kingdom of God," Jesus said. Nicodemus saith unto him, How can a man be born when he is old? Can he enter the second time into his mother's womb, and be born? Jesus answered, Except a man be born of water and of the Spirit, he cannot enter into the kingdom of God. That which is born of the flesh is flesh; and that which is born of the Spirit is spirit. Marvel not that I said unto thee, Ye must be born again. If I have told you earthly things, and ye believe not, how shall ye believe, if I tell you of heavenly things? And no man hath ascended up to heaven, but he that came down from heaven, even the Son of man which is in heaven." Then Jesus speaks of his own death on the cross, "even so must the Son of man be lifted up: That whosoever believeth in him should not perish, but have eternal life." [3:1-16]

Natural man is born and lives physically — but he is under the sin curse. He is actually "dead [spiritually speaking] in his trespasses and sin." And he will stay dead for eternity and forever separated from God his creator unless something happens. It did God's only begotten son — the Son of Man descended from Heaven. Born of a virgin just as the prophets of old said it would happen; grew and waxed strong; taught and preached the Gospe [good news] of God's plan of salvation; then "lifted up" on the cross to pay man's penalty for sin. "The wages of sin is death," the Bible says. We all have a sin debt we cannot pay, "but the gift of God is eternal life." Jesus paid the debt for us. Bought us [that means redeemed us] with His own blood. He arose from the dead the third day as he said he would; met with and gave his followers "To whom also he shewed himself alive after his passing by many infallible proofs, being seen of them forty days, and speaking of the things pertaining to the kingdom of God:" And then he ascended back to Heaven with a sure promise of His return for them.

We have in Acts 1: "And when he had spoken these things, while they beheld, he was taken up; and a cloud received him out of their sight. And while they looked steadfastly toward heaven as he went up, behold, two men stood by them in white apparel; Which also said, Ye men of Galilee, why stand ye gazing up into heaven? this same Jesus, which is taken up from you into heaven, shall so come in like manner as ye have seen him go into heaven."

Acts 4:12 says: "Neither is there salvation in any other: for there is none other name under heaven given among men, whereby we must be saved." Often called the "Gospel in Miniature" John 3:16 says: "For God so loved the world that He gave his only begotten son that whosoever believes in Him shall not perish but have everlasting life."

So humans who hear this Gospel and believe it by faith and repent [turn to God for forgiveness of sin] will never perish. Their name is written down in glory as a permanent citizen of Heaven. The old hymn on the next page says it well:

There's A New Name
Written Down In Glory

I was once a sinner, but I came
Pardon to receive from my Lord:
This was freely given, and I found
That He always kept His word.

There's a new name written down in glory,
And it's mine, O yes, it's mine!
And the white robed angels sing the story,
"A sinner has come home."

For there's a new name written down in glory,
And it's mine, O yes, it's mine!
With my sins forgiven I am bound for Heaven,
Never more to roam.

I was humbly kneeling at the cross,
Fearing naught but God's angry frown;
When the heavens opened and I saw
That my name was written down.

In the Book 'tis written, "Saved by Grace,"
O the joy that came to my soul!
Now I am forgiven, and I know
By the blood I am made whole.

Fascinated with God's creatures — the fast and the slow.

CHAPTER 7

The Daring Rescue

This leads us to the second of the four liberating truths I began to share a chapter or so back. I wrote how that when I first met Sadie she was covered with seed ticks. I was raised in the country. I thought I knew everything there was to know about ticks and hound dogs. But I didn't have the slightest on seed ticks and how dangerous they are until we took Sadie for that first vet visit and learned she had already been seriously impacted by these harmless-looking little specks.

Sometimes in the Bible, the disease of leprosy is used to illustrate sin. Named Hansen's Disease or HD after the man that identified its nature back in 1873, is a chronic infection that primarily affects the peripheral nerves, skin, upper respiratory tract, eyes, and nasal mucosa. The disease is caused by a bacillus (rod-shaped) bacterium known as Mycobacterium leprae, a slow-growing, intracellular pathogen that cannot live outside its host — animal or human. We usually associate the ancient disease with that impacting humans. In Bible times, lepers were ordered separated from family and community. Those with leprosy were grotesque to the sight and by law had to cry out "unclean, unclean" when someone approached. If a Jew was healed, he or she had to be examined by a priest and declared clean before integrating again into society. So like leprosy, sin brings separation, suffering and shame — that's the application.

But I have another one — seed ticks. Ticks, disease carrying parasites are like sin. We have had one of the most rainy summers in history in Oklahoma this year. There is an over abundance of ticks. The life cycle of a tick is composed of four stages: egg, larval, nymphal and adult. It is the larvae that is commonly referred to as seed ticks. They hatch from the eggs of an adult female tick and are very tiny. As such, they are rarely noticeable unless found in large groups. Those falling off of my pup at the vet's resembled poppy seeds with six legs.

If you are like me, right now you are probably checking and scratching your scalp. If Sadie knew what I was conveying here, she would have that back leg scratching at her neck 90 miles an hour or chomping her belly and back with her teeth.

Now, keep in mind I am not putting together an informational sheet on ticks, but rather offering a lesson on the nature of sin which is like seed ticks. After hatching, seed ticks immediately look for a host — something with blood. They will feed on the first suitable host they find. [Keep in mind these are things about ticks in which we can make a spiritual application. Sin is looking for a willing host].

Seed ticks remain attached to their hosts for as long as they can before dropping. In some cases, a tick will reattach itself to the same host after entering the nymphal stage. [Reminds me of that short parable Jesus tells in Luke 11:24-26 about the "evil spirit that comes out of a man, it goes through arid places seeking rest and does not find it. Then it says, "I will return to the house I left." When it arrives, it finds the house swept clean and put in order. Then it goes and takes seven other spirits more wicked than itself, and they go in and live there. And the final condition of that man is worse than the first."

Some tick species, such as the winter tick, remain attached to one host throughout their lives. [Keep that one in mind when I get to the Truth No. 3 about Christians who "have to sin."] Seed ticks some- times die if they cannot locate a suitable host. However, seed ticks are capable of surviving for long periods of time without a meal.

In the Epistle of James we have the half brother of Jesus writing under direction of the Holy Spirit "Then when lust hath conceived, it bringeth forth sin: and sin, when it is finished, bringeth forth death." What a picture of the advance of the seed tick. Had we not taken action on Sadie's behalf, her time on earth would have been short and all the delightful times we've had would not have been.

Likewise, sin advances toward its goal — death. Sin is terminal. More than one preacher has used Christian apologist Ravi Zachar- ias' description of what sin will always do: "Sin will take you further than you want to go; make you stay longer than you want to stay; and always make you pay more than you want to pay," he writes.

The Bible says "The wages of sin is death."

"But my sins are small," we might protest. The thing about little sins is that they are like seed ticks, they grow up very fast.

"One who has a light view of sin never has great thoughts of God," another Christian author, C.S. Lewis writes.

For my dog, the tick issue had to be addressed. We listened to the vet, bought and applied the medicine and developed a preven tive to keep the ticks from returning.

"I'm telling you Sadie Sue, that'll preach," I said as Sadie came to see what I was working on at the computer and nudged me with her nose. Sometimes, we just have to take time out to play.

One other application before I move on: For the believer, sin is the same way as those little seed ticks — almost as hard to see as the leprosy creating bacteria. If not dealt with we are overtaken and life here and life to come is forever impacted. Just as we rescued Sadie from her ticks et al, Jesus rescued us from sin. He was on a rescue mission when He came to this earth to "seek and to save that which was lost."

"So master, why did the Creator make ticks and fleas and mosquitos and poison ivy and such in the first place . . . and will there be ticks in Heaven?" Sadie asks.

"Well, Sadie this could be another rabbit chase. Let me say first of all, that when you said 'first place' I heard it a little differently than the way you asked the question. I'm not sure ticks were there in that 'first place' or for that matter, will be in the final place. If they are, then they will function in harmony with God's creation to fulfill the Creator's purpose.

But let me offer why I believe there will not be any thorn trees in the new Heaven and the new Earth. We know there has been a lot of changes in creature and creation since the fall of man and the subsequent judgements of God including the Great Flood.

"I believe there is plenty of Bible evidence to prove the elimination of bad germs, bad insects, bad weather, bad animals and bad people. In this book we are dealing with people and animals, but let me at least offer two principle ideas from "the Word." In Revelation 21 we have, "But there shall by no means enter it [the made new place] anything that defiles." Further, we are told, "And God shall wipe away all tears from their eyes; and there shall be no more death, neither sorrow, nor crying, neither shall there be any more pain: for the former things are passed away."

"So Sadie, no ticks there. At least not as we know ticks in this present dispensation."

"Well I like that idea, master. No dips either, huh?"

"Hmmmm . . . guess not," I answer.

A couple of other things in that regard before we get back to "those four liberating truths." Remember, in the beginning — before the fall — neither humans nor animals experienced death, disease or decay. Because of the fall of man, animals would take on a new role. They would be killed for sacrifice, eaten for food. Their coats would be used for clothing, shelter and containers. Their bones for tools and weaponry. That was not so in the beginning and one day will no longer be so. These are critical points as we contemplate the coming kingdom and how that animals were originally created not to sustain mankind but to bring pleasure as companions to man and glory to God their creator.

A kingdom, a Heaven, a restored paradise, a golden age, a utopia without plants and animals?

I don't think so.

C

Sadie is one great "watch" dog! And loves to ride and go fishing.

CHAPTER 8

The Truth Will Set You Free

Truth No. 2: Because of what Jesus has done for us in "The Rescue" those who have been saved [rescued] will never die. Better said, they will die no more. A believer dies only one time. Let me explain. When Adam and Eve were told not to eat of the tree of good and evil or they would die, what was being referenced was a spiritual death and ultimately a physical death. Then there will be a "second death" — a final destination for the soul that rejects Christ. "And death and hell were cast into the lake of fire. This is the second death," the Bible says in Revelation 20:14.

There are no more "get out of jail free cards" as one man describes opportunities and invitations for people to accept Christ as their only hope in this world and the world to come. There is a rescuer, a redeemer — yea, a savior. We cannot reject Jesus in this life and hope for any different outcome. And contrary to what some seem to teach and believe, God is not going to drag those into Heaven kicking and screaming who do not want to go there.

"Whosoever shall call upon the name of the Lord shall be saved," is used three times in the Bible—once in Joel 2:32 as par of a prophetic account, once in Acts 2:21 by the Apostle Peter during his address at Pentecost, and once in Romans 10:13 by the Apostle Paul in his letter. When the jailer in Phillipi asked the disciples "What must I do to be saved?" they answered "Believe in the Lord Jesus, and you will be saved -- you and your household." Acts 16:31 [By the way, I wonder if he had any pets in the house?]

The point I want to make: It is not the call alone that brings salvation but rather the believing [trusting] in the one that is being called upon. ". . . if you shall confess with your mouth the Lord Jesus, and shall believe in your heart that God has raised him from the dead, you shall be saved." — Romans 10:9

Those who never bend the knee to Christ in this life to accept [receives] Him as their savior are defined as dead. We all are born with that death sentence. The Bible tells us we are dead people. Physically alive but dead spiritually. Jesus said "let the dead bury the dead." — Luke 6:90. We are "dead in our trespasses and sin." — Ephesians 2:1. The light comes but men love darkness. — John 3:19. We read further in Romans 1. "For the invisible things of him from the creation of the world are clearly seen, being understood by the things that are made, even his eternal power and Godhead; so that they are without excuse: Because that, when they knew God, they glorified him not as God, neither were thankful; but became vain in their imaginations, and their foolish heart was darkened. Professing themselves to be wise, they became fools." (20-22).

So they are dead spiritually and then they die physically. Jesus said "fear not them which kill the body, but are not able to kill the soul: but rather fear him which is able to destroy both soul and body in hell." — Matthew 10:28. Spiritually, we are going to spend eternity somewhere.

But for the believer, physical death is described as simply leaving the physical body behind for a time — the Bible calls it "absent from the body and present with the Lord." That is the current state of all who have died and gone to be with Jesus . . . and waiting for the glorious resurrection.

The Bible says in 1st Corinthians 15 "now is Christ risen from the dead, and become the firstfruits of them that slept. For since by man came death, by man came also the resurrection of the dead. For as in Adam all die, even so in Christ shall all be made alive. But every man in his own order: Christ the firstfruits; afterward they that are Christ's at his coming. Then cometh the end, when he shall have delivered up the kingdom to God, even the Father; when he shall have put down all rule and all authority and power."

When I say it is a great truth that "Christians only die once," I am not talking about the physical death since we see that for the Christian that transaction is identified as leaving the physical body and going to heaven in a spiritual body. "O death, where is your sting? O grave, where is your victory?" is the taunting question in verse 55.

So the death I am talking about is the dying to self, receiving Christ and being born of the Spirit. The new birth. Then we can say with the Apostle the promise and principle that is ours in the New Testament: "I am crucified with Christ: nevertheless I live; yet not I, but Christ lives in me: and the life which I now live in the flesh I live by the faith of the Son of God, who loved me, and gave himself for me." — Galatians 2:20.

OK, let me briefly touch on the third great truth I find so liberating in this life.

Truth No. 3: "Believers do not have to sin." [Clue, we sin because we want to, not because we have to sin.] I'll come back here in a moment, but first let me set up the fourth great truth.

Truth No. 4: "Grace-provided eternity is most important thing of all. It is this fourth one that provides the basis for all I have to say about why I believe we will have our pets with us in eternity — why I believe that when the rapture and first resurrection occur at the Second Coming of Christ animals, including my Beagle Sadie, will be part of the equation.

So briefly about Truth No. 3, there is a teaching that is repeated much too often in and around our Christian fellowships [notice I did not say churches, lest someone think about the building on the corner instead of the local body of believers]. I hesitate to say false teaching, although I believe it is dangerously close. This idea that somehow it is an expected or a natural thing for Christians to sin.

I am afraid that we are so anxious to appeal to Romans 7:14-21 to justify our losing struggles with sin and living far below God's best for our lives, that we miss the greater truths found in the same area of our Bibles, some in the same chapter. First read the often cited verses that we hear by those who seem to be telling us that it is normal for Christians to sin . [To be sure I'm clear, I am using New Living Translation]: The Apostle Paul is teaching about the law of sin — how it works and the impossibilities of having victory over sin if we live in the flesh.

"So the trouble is not with the law, for it is spiritual and good. The trouble is with me, for I am all too human, a slave to sin. I don't really understand myself, for I want to do what is right, but I don't do it. Instead, I do what I hate. But if I know that what I am doing is wrong, this shows that I agree that the law is good. So I am not the one doing wrong; it is sin living in me that does it. And I know that nothing good lives in me, that is, in my sinful nature. I want to do what is right, but I can't. I want to do what is good, but I don't. I don't want to do what is wrong, but I do it anyway. But if

I do what I don't want to do, I am not really the one doing wrong; it is sin living in me that does it. I have discovered this principle of life — that when I want to do what is right, I inevitably do what is wrong."

Question: Did we forget what we read just a few verses back? Romans 7:4-6 "So, my dear brothers and sisters, this is the point: You died to the power of the law when you died with Christ. And now you are united with the one who was raised from the dead. As a result, we can produce a harvest of good deeds for God. When we were con- trolled by our old nature, sinful desires were at work within us, and the law aroused these evil desires that produced a harvest of sinful deeds, resulting in death. But now we have been released from the law, for we died to it and are no longer captive to its power. Now we can serve God, not in the old way of obeying the letter of the law, but in the new way of living in the Spirit.

And a little further back yet. Remember the Apostle's question in Romans 6:1-2: "What shall we say then? Shall we continue in sin, that grace may abound? God forbid. How shall we, that are dead to sin, live any longer therein?

The fact is, and this is why it is so important to include it here, I am not talking about Christians reaching a state of holiness in this life called "sinless perfection," but rather than fall again and again into worldly sin and carnality, live a victorious lifestyle in which we are ready at any moment to be whisked away by Christ and to the Judge- ment seat of Christ. Someone has well coined the phrase "rapture ready."

When Jesus saved us He not only saved us from the Penalty of sin, but he saved us from the Power of sin. One day we will be re moved from the Presence of sin.

"If there are no dogs in Heaven, then when I die I want to go where they went."

—Will Rogers

At left, Will tries his hand at the linotype machine. At right he uses his always handy typewriter to pen another column.

CHAPTER 9

Waiting for Us There

OK, one might say, but all this has to do with humans — the re-generation of people who have heard the Gospel and responded in the positive way. Our loved ones who have "died in Christ," Christians have gone to Heaven and are waiting for us there. We get it. But what of our pets that have parted? Will they be waiting for us there?

I believe so. People go to Heaven because they have believed the Gospel — good news that Jesus is the Christ who paid their sin debt by dying on the cross. He arose from the dead and is coming a second time. That is what the Bible says. They have believed it and called on Christ through faith. Grace and mercy have been extended. "For by grace are ye saved through faith; and that not of yourselves: it is the gift of God:," Ephesians 2:8.

But how does that work with our pets? How do animals repent exercise faith and believe the Gospel? They don't. God did no create them with that capacity. Animals, remember are programec to function and respond to God's creation even under the sin curse brought on by the humans. They are basically innocent. In that regard we find animals as types in the Biblical narrative. Christ himself is referred to as "the Lamb" from Genesis to Revelation. The seriousness of man's rebellion against God and the absolute need for atonement is shown in the killing and sacrificing of animals — the innocent dying for the guilty. "Without the shedding of blood," the Bible says, "there is no remission." — Heb. 9:22. And further, pointing to the supreme sacrifice that must be paid to satisfy the penalty for sin, "It is impossible for the blood of bulls and goats to take away sins," Heb. 10. 4. It had to be Christ dying on the cross atoning for our sins.

All of redemption then is through the same finished work of Christ and it is all by grace. In Genesis 6:7 we read: "And the LORD said, I will destroy man whom I have created from the face of the earth; both man, and beast, and the creeping thing, and the fowls of the air; for it repents me that I have made them." And in the NET version: "So the LORD said, "I will wipe humankind, whom I have created, from the face of the earth -- everything from humankind to animals, including creatures that move on the ground and birds of the air, for I regret that I have made them." Then in the next verse we have: "But Noah found grace in the eyes of the LORD."

Well guess who else found grace in the eyes of the Lord in the wake of the pending Flood?

Animals. Companions to humans often abused by the ones who were supposed to be their caretakers. Then as in the Garden, they were innocent of the wicked rebellion against God.

Animals are not called on to repent [turn from sin] and believe.

Yes, I know we have an instance in Jonah where the animals are caused to fast and wear sackcloth after the prophet began to announce the coming judgement. "Then the people of Nineveh believed in God; and they called a fast and put on sackcloth from the greatest to the least of them." The king of Nineveh issued a proclamation "Do not let man, beast, herd, or flock taste a thing. Do not let them eat or drink water . . . both man and beast must be covered with sackcloth; and let men call on God earnestly that each may turn from his wicked way and from the violence which is in his hands. Who knows, God may turn and relent and withdraw His burning anger so that we will not perish." — Jonah 3:5-9.

Notice, however men are to call on God, not the animals. Jonah 3:5-9. It seems the worldly king of Nineveh was serious enough about repentance, however, to include the animals in the fast.

Animals for sure are recipients of God's grace. Grace is more than an attribute of a just and loving God. It is His sovereign character that takes into account the innocent and the guilty. Man is guilty. Even Noah and the other seven humans on the Ark were guilty. Unlike those that perished in the flood, they responded to God's invitation to get on the ark. That's why the Ark is a type of Christ. Jesus is our "ark of safety." The Ark was a grace-fueled rescue mission for humans and innocent animals .

Like babies and children before they reach the age of accountability [not sure when that is. I have seen some eight-year-olds organizing crime] and those who do not have capacity, animals are in the pale of God's grace. Yes, innocent animals and even human infants and toddlers lost their physical lives in the flood. I'm not sure how all of that works out but I do know God is good, gracious and just. For animals — as reflected in the Genesis account — there is a careful continuum.

So will you meet your pets in eternity? Will my beagle go with me in the rapture? I can tell you that as this manuscript is readied for the publisher Sadie and I are still on planet earth. What we expect to happen is one of two things — maybe better stated one of three possible things. We will be going along one day — running, walking, sleeping — in the boat, or riding in the pickup. The trump will sound and in a moment, the twinkling of an eye, we will be "caught away" [raptured].

Or, one of us dies and goes on to heaven to await the other; or both of us die and go to heaven to await a time when our spiritual bodies are reunited with our permanent physical bodies and ultimate- ly return to earth for the millennium reign of Christ.

Premillennialism is the belief that Jesus Christ will physically return to the earth before "The Millennium" as specifically cited in chapter 20 of the New Testament Book of Revelation. The "return" is referred to as the Second Coming and is in two stages. The first part can occur at any time. We call this "the rapture." It is the catching away of the saints [believers in Christ] living at that time and the resurrected bodies of believers. The raptured will be changed, and the resurrected will be glorified and reunited with their souls returning with Christ. Collectively with Christ there is a return then to Heaven for a seven-year period at which time the Tribulation takes place on the earth, the Antichrist comes to power and the world readies for the Battle of Armageddon. At the end of the seven-year period, Christ and the believers with glorified bodies return to earth victoriously to rule and reign for 1000 years — the Millennium. Premillennialism is distinct from the other [less-literal] forms of eschatology such as postmillennialism or amillennialism, which view the millennial rule as occurring either before the second coming, or as being figurative and non-temporal. Again, premillennialism is based upon a literal interpretation of Revelation 20:1–6 which describes Jesus' coming to the earth and subsequent reign at the end of an apocalyptic period of tribulation. There, as throughout the Bible, there is a time of fulfillment for the prophetic hope of God's people as given in the Old Testament.

CHAPTER 10

Hounds Going to Heaven?

Remember Rod Sterling's Twilight Zone? There's an episode "The Hunt" from the early sixties [I saw it in living black and white] about a coon hunter who dies with his hound. They have been trans- lated to a field and as they walk along they come to a gate. As they approach they are met by the keeper who won't let his dog come in with his master who remarks: "It just don't seem right" and if his dog isn't allowed to come with him he will just keep on walking. Then the man and the hound comes to another gate in which the hunter tells the keeper what happened down the road. "With no dogs allowed, it must be a helluva heaven," is about what the old guy said. It turns out in Twilight Zone fashion that Hell is exactly the place that was behind that first gate. "Of course", he was told, "All dogs are allowed in Heaven."

Of course, we who feel blessed of God to love and be loved by dogs [cats; or other pets] we amen that story. However, we do well and honor the God who gave us our animals if we have an attitude like my dog Sadie. When she was questioning me about what might be in heaven to cause her to want to go there — squirrels, grass and mole hills? — she concludes, "Master, if you're going to be there then that's where i want to be." For the believer, the greatest thing in Heaven is not going to be some relative, person, pet or pleasure. It's going to be the presence of the Master.

Just so readers of "Will My Beagle Go With Me In The Rapture? won't think I am the only Christian author who believes pets will be in Heaven (animals in the Kingdom to come, if you will) here are names of some very credible other writers that agree:

Randy Alcorn in his book simply called "Heaven" writes that he believes animals will be present in the Kingdom of Heaven. Other authors who believe that pets go to heaven include: C.S. Lewis, Peter Kreeft, Niki Behrikis Shanahan and James Herriot. Many pastors, theologians, and other Christian giants believe it so — from the not so orthodox to the very orthodox. Famous fundamentalist leaders like John R. Rice, H.A. Inside, and Lee Roberson preached and wrote about Heaven as the "Sweet Home of Departed Saints" and of a millennial kingdom that would roll into an eternity populated by all of God's creatures.

Jesus said: "In my Father's house are many mansions: if it were not so, I would have told you. I go to prepare a place for you." — John 14:2. Can you imagine a heavenly future prepared by Christ the Creator void of His marvelous creation of rocks and hills and plants and flowers . . . and animals? Or going home to a "home" void of our pets who have loved us so unconditionally and always happy to see us so much so they can hardly contain it — jumping around, twisting, licking, barking, rubbing and rolling around?

Suffice it to say many believe that pets do go to heaven and that there will be animals in a future kingdom — a new heaven and a new earth.

But what does the Bible say?

We know that both humans and animals were formed from the ground. "Now the Lord God had formed out of the ground all the beasts of the field and all the birds of the air" (Genesis 2:19).

Alcorn's work makes a good case for dogs having souls.

"When God breathed a spirit into Adam's body, made from the earth, Adam became nephesh, a "living being" or "soul" (Genesis 2:7). Remarkably, the same Hebrew word, nephesh, is used for animals and for people. We are specifically told that not only people, but animals have "the breath of life" in them (Genesis 1:30, 2:7, 6:17, 7:15, 22). God hand-made animals, linking them both to the earth and humanity."

Alcorn emphasizes (and this author agrees) that animals and humans are definitely distinct from each other and that animals do not have human souls. Animals aren't created in God's image, and they aren't equal to human in any sense.

"Nonetheless," he says, "there's a strong biblical case for animals having nonhuman souls."

Alcorn said he didn't take such seriously until he studied the usage of the Hebrew and Greek words nephesh and psyche, often translated "soul" when referring to humans. (Nephesh is translated psyche in the Septuagint.) Alcorn says that the use of these words for animals is more "compelling evidence" that they have nonhuman souls.

"It wasn't until the advent of seventeenth-century Enlightenment . . . that the existence of animal souls was even questioned in Western civilization," say Gary Habermas and J.P. Moreland in their book, Beyond Death. "Throughout the history of the church, the classic understanding of living things has included the doctrine that animals, as well as humans, have souls."

There are a lot of famous people who have weighed in on the

question about where dogs go when they die, whether or not they have souls, and if there could be a special heaven for dogs. Well, as we have said earlier, there are almost as many differing opinions as there are people. So we always want to go to the One Source we can count on for truth.

That said, many of us share at least some of the sentiment expressed by the following renown folk. One of the favorite quotes is by the man who may have read more newspaper than Holy Writ . . . Oklahoma's most native son, Will Rogers (actor, writer, roper, humorist).

"If there are no dogs in Heaven," Will said. "then when I die I want to go where they went."

Then there is author Mark Twain's (Samuel Clemons) assertion: "Heaven goes by favor. If it went by merit, you would stay out and your dog would go in."

Some Other Good Quotes About Dogs

"You can say any foolish thing to a dog, and the dog will give you a look that says, 'Wow, you're right! I never would've thought of that!'" —Dave Barry (columnist).

"A dog is the only thing on earth that loves you more than he loves himself."

—Josh Billings (a.k.a. Henry Wheeler Shaw; humorist and lecturer) "Dogs are not our whole life, but they make our lives whole."

—Roger Caras (photographer and writer)

"Dogs are wise. They crawl away into a quiet corner and lick their wounds and do not rejoin the world until they are whole once more." —Agatha Christie (author)

"The better I get to know men, the more I find myself loving dogs." —Charles de Gaulle (former President of the French Republic)

"What counts is not necessarily the size of the dog in the fight; it's the size of the fight in the dog."

—Dwight D. Eisenhower (34th President of the United States)

"There are three faithful friends: an old wife, an old dog, and ready money."

—Benjamin Franklin (A Founding Father of the United States)

"Once you have had a wonderful dog, a life without one, is a life diminished."

—Dean Koontz (author)

"Don't accept your dog's admiration as conclusive evidence that you are wonderful."

—Ann Landers (advice columnist)

"I care not for a man's religion whose dog and cat are not the better for it."

—Abraham Lincoln (16th President of the United States)

"No one appreciates the very special genius of your conversation as the dog does."

—Christopher Morley (author)

"I think dogs are the most amazing creatures; they give uncondition- al love. For me, they are the role model for being alive."

—Gilda Radner (comedienne)

"The average dog is a nicer person than the average person." — Andy Rooney (contributor, 60 Minutes)

"Happiness is a warm puppy." —Charles M. Schulz (cartoonist, Peanuts)

"I've seen a look in dogs' eyes, a quickly vanishing look of amazed contempt, and I am convinced that basically dogs think humans are nuts." —John Steinbeck (author, The Grapes of Wrath)

"You think dogs will not be in heaven? I tell you, they will be there long before any of us."

—Robert Louis Stevenson (author, Treasure Island)

"If I have any beliefs about immortality, it is that certain dogs I have known will go to heaven, and very, very few persons." — James Thurber (author, "The Secret Life of Walter Mitty")

"If you want a friend in Washington, get a dog." —Harry S. Truman (33rd President of the United States)

"If a dog will not come to you after having looked you in the face, you should go home and examine your conscience."

—Woodrow Wilson (28th President of the United States)

CHAPTER 11

Did Snoopy Make It?

In John Bunyan's 17th century classic, Pilgrim's Progress, at the Wicket Gate, Christian is directed onto the "straight and narrow" King's Highway by the gatekeeper Goodwill [Jesus] who saves him from Beelzebub's archers and shows him the heavenly way he must go. Along a road filled with all kinds of spiritual terrors, Christian confronts the characters of Worldly Wiseman, Giant Despair, Talkative, Ignorance, and the demons of the Valley of the Shadow of Death. But Christian completes his journey and arrives in the Celestial City.

"So Sadie," I said one day as we walked in the park. "I want to talk about our journey to Heaven."

There is much information about "heaven" based on fantasy, fairy tales, crazy cartoons, television series and hollywood theology. I saw one episode of "Highway to Heaven" that even had a dog die and become an angel.

"Loving Master?" Sadie asks, "when I look up there beyond the tops of these oaks where the tree rabbits jump and play . . . and I look out there where the birds are flying, is that heaven? And those things that look like cotton balls . . . clouds, right?"

"Well yes, Sadie, those are clouds," I answer. (You can see we've been working on vocabulary.) "And yes that is one heaven. Farther out, there are suns and moons and planets. Thats another heaven. But the Bible talks about a third heaven. That's the one we're talking about here."

"And did you say tree rabbits Sadie?"

"Seems to me, Sadie, you have a "Snoopy" kind of way of bringing some great comic relief when I get too serious or too heavy."

"Well, I am a beagle, don't you know?" Sadie comes back.

"No, we're not going up there to float around on clouds in our white bath robes playing harps day in and day out," I say, trying to recapture the seriousness of the matter.

"Well what are we going to do up there, Loving Master?" Sadie wonders.

"Well Sadie, that is yet another good question. A lot of humans ask the same thing," I explain. "These are some of the things we're answering in this book."

"Master, I know you expect a lot out of me, but I don't sense I can read," Sadie says. "You're just going to have to tell me."

"Alright Sadie. You win," I say. "We're just going to make this our comic relief chapter. Which by the way (and in keeping with our theme and chapter heading) there will be some humor and laughing in Heaven. I don't know about cartoon characters per se, but maybe their creators. I mean after all, I don't expect to see as many prune face believers as we see today."

"Sadie, did you mean to say you don't think you can read?"

"No, Loving Master. Dogs don't think, they sense. Isn't that what you said?' she asked. "You've still got a lot to learn about dogs, Loving Master."

"Good night, Sadie, I'm 60+ years old and here I am trying to learn from a dog?"

"Well, you know what they say, don't you LM?" "What's that?" "You can't teach an old dog new tricks."

"Now Sadie, that's funny. You're a comic dog." "You mean like Snoopy?"

"Sadie, slow down. Seems like you know an awful lot about a lot of things for a two-year-old beagle. Are you talking about the most famous Beagle in the world — truly a comic beagle?"

"Well, two things LM. You remember when we were talking about famous quotes and you were taking pride in your life as a newspaperman?"

"Yes, I remember. And you know what Sadie? Sometimes when you repeat this stuff back to me I hear it in a different light — sometimes it's rather convicting too. Didn't mean to come across as prideful? I am reminded of what The Bible says: "For all that is in the world, the lust of the flesh, and the lust of the eyes, and the pride of life, is not of the Father, but is of the world." 1st John 2:16.

"And what's this about old? Sixty-plus is not old," I protest. "Just wait until I tell you how dog and human years equate. Why Sadie did you know that in human years you are only two? But in dog years, you're already a teenager?

"Maybe that accounts for some of your rebellion?"

"And what's this LM thing? Are you renaming me?"

"Well, Loving Master, you're the one dropping names and shortening names . . . and sometimes giving names. You just made up a name for that gruffly old dog on the corner across from the park entrance. His name is not 'Old Deep Bark.'"

"OK Sadie, I get it. But does not 'Old Deep Bark' sound better than 'Gruffly Old Dog?'

"Now what about that famous quotes thing?"

"That one about Will Rogers. You suggested he should have read more of what you call The Book instead of so many newspapers and if he had, maybe he would have known more about Heaven.

"He's also the one who said "All I know is what I read in the papers. Well, that's like me LM. The only thing I know comes from information you share with me. So my famous quote can be "'All I know is what my master tells me.'"

"Very good, Sadie. Another good life lesson for rearing dogs and kids," I said. "Two things: First I would never want it to stand that I faulted someone as great as Will Rogers.

He was one of God's gifts to this world — and what I was trying to say is that he was a tremendous dog lover and proved it with that quote about if dogs had their own heaven then he would choose that heaven instead of one with only humans. If only I had just a little bit of his wit and way with words."

William Penn Adair "Will" Rogers (Nov. 4, 1879 – Aug. 15, 1935) is Oklahoma's favorite son. Not far from where Sadie and I live there is a Memorial to him at Claremore, Okla. Just north is his boyhood home. There, Will learned to cowboy. He especially became good with handling a rope. Doing rope tricks would open other doors. Rogers became a vaudeville performer and ultimately a movie star. He also was a humorist, newspaper columnist and wise-cracking social commentator —l probably the most famous American media star during the 1920s and 1930s. He made more than 70 movies (50 silent films and 21 "talkies") and wrote more than 4,000 nationally syndicated newspaper columns. Sources agree that at the time of his death he was world famous, the leading political wit of his time, and the highest paid star in Hollywood. Rogers died in 1935 with aviator Wiley Post when their small airplane crashed in northern Alaska.

"As for Snoopy? Yes he was [and still is] a famous beagle creat- ed by cartoonist Charles Schulz. I read somewhere that Schulz ac- tually came up with Snoopy from his childhood experiences and the cartoon beagle may be a combination of several of his pets.

"At any rate, Sadie, Mr. Schulz used his beagle to convey mes- sages to his audience, and in a sense that's what we're doing here. Snoopy spoke (actually thought) through those bubble panels above his head. And here, we have you using human conversation. So Snoopy is a good role model for you."

Snoopy of course was prone to imagining fantasy lives, includ- ing that of a World War One flying Ace. Snoopy is a great pre- tender. He pretends to be college student "Joe Cool," and even imagines himself a writer."

"Kind of like you, LM?"

"Now Sadie, that was below the belt."

"What's that mean, LM?"

"Never mind. You're always getting me off focus — chasing rabbits again."

"Now. that's something we can talk about master. I'm a Beagle.

"When I tree a squirrel, my bark sounds like that of a Walker Hound. Other times, I just sound like a common dog, but as I heard you telling someone the other day, LM, when I'm chasing rabbits, there is no doubt about it, it's a beagle bark. I am all the way beagle."

"Yes you are, Sadie Sue. I can argue for that. You are the real issue. No pretending there. But if you get to be haughty I will sing you that song you like."

"What song is that master?"

"You ain't nothin' but a hound dog, cryin' all the time, you ain't never caught a rabbit and you ain't no friend of mine."

"Oooooh pleeeze!" Sadie whines. [Like I said, this is our comic relief chapter.]

"Well anyway, about Snoopy of the comic strip. He's a great pretender. He fantasizes higher than he can reach. He want's to be something he's not and fails. His short "novels" never get published, and as a WWI Fighting Ace his imaginary enemy, the Red Baron, always shoots him down.

"Snoopy cannot talk, so his thoughts are in those balloons — not verbalized. His moods are conveyed much like yours through growls, sighs, little yaps and full blown high pitch barks.

"Here's the difference, Sadie. We're having lots of fun with our interaction and our pretended conversation, but our subject matter is as real and sincere as a ride in the pickup, treeing a squirrel, digging up a mole, clipping along the water in a bass boat or going great guns after a rabbit.

"Heaven is for real!"

"Isn't that the name of a book or a movie LM?"

"Why, yes it is Sadie. Movies, books? Really out of your realm there Sadie Sue! But speaking of such, the "Peanuts Movie" is at the theater. Now Sadie is welcome at Atwoods Farm Store, Westlakes Hardware and Lowes, but we haven't tried the theater.

Does Sadie watch movies? Well sometimes we think so.

"You was pretty fascinated with 'Marmaduke' hey Sadie?"

"Sure was Master. All those dogs could talk . . . and there was a neat beagle in the cast."

No caption needed! (Make up your own).

CHAPTER 12

Christ Coming for the Saved

What in the world is "the rapture?' I suppose that if I am to answer the question as proposed in the title of this work, "Will My Beagle Go With Me In The Rapture?" I best be about defining the term "rapture."

There is a future event coming in history known as the Second Coming of Christ. I say future event because there are those who teach that it has already occurred — in 70 A.D. they suppose. There are others that would tell you that the second advent has to do with your coming to faith in Christ. Neither of those views make any sense when exposed to plain reading of the scripture.

Here is what the Bible says about the Second Coming and the rapture: "But I would not have you to be ignorant, brethren, concerning them which are asleep, that ye sorrow not, even as others which have no hope. For if we believe that Jesus died and rose again, even so them also which sleep in Jesus will God bring with him. For this we say unto you by the word of the Lord, that we which are alive and remain unto the coming of the Lord shall not prevent them which are asleep. For the Lord himself shall descend from heaven with a shout, with the voice of the archangel, and with the trump of God: and the dead in Christ shall rise first: Then we which are alive and remain shall be caught up together with them in the clouds, to meet the Lord in the air: and so shall we ever be with the Lord. Wherefore comfort one another with these words."

— 1 Thessalonians 4:13-18

So briefly, we have talked about the Garden. In the beginning God made everything. He made the universe, the suns, moons and planets. He made the rocks and the elements that they are formed of; the water and the gasses and everything it takes to make them all work together. He made the plants, the insects, the fish, the birds, the animals big and small.

"He made cats and dogs and the sounds they make," I tell Sadie. "He made their senses and a knowledge of how to interact with each other and their environment. And he made humans — the first man, Adam, and the first woman, Eve. And he placed them in this beautiful garden where they could all live together and have friendship, fellow- ship, relationship with each other and with their creator God — forever if they chose."

All of creation was in harmony with God's plan it seemed. But unlike with his other creatures, God made man a free moral agent — with intellect, reasoning powers and decision making abilities to act out on information. Not programed like robots or with instinct like animals. He didn't make us with built-in Global Positioning Systems, computers, compasses, telescopes or microscopes, but with the capacity and capability of discovering such things. In His own image, creativity and appreciation for the fruit of that creativity. But even with all of the freedom up to and including rejection of the One who made them and loves them supremely, God's permissive will still does not allow man to become his own god without dire circumstances.

God had placed a prohibition on one tree and its fruit. He told the man in Genesis 2:17 "But of the tree of the knowledge of good and evil, you shall not eat of it: for in the day that you eat thereof you shall surely die."

When Satan in the form of a serpent made his appeal to Eve it was that one temptation that drew her and her husband from God's "plan and purpose." He does the same today. First of all, causing us to doubt God's Word as authentic and authoritative, then telling us we "are the captains of our own fate." We surely know more than God. "You," the atheist says, "are your own gods."

"You shall not surely die," Satan told the woman. "For God doth know that in the day ye eat thereof, then your eyes shall be opened, and ye shall be as gods [God], knowing good and evil." Gen. 3:4-5

Well, we know what happened. Man sinned against God and was driven from the Garden. Because of man's transgression, all of creation would suffer. Death and decay entered into an environment that would otherwise have been kept in perfect generation. Each kingdom was impacted downward — the animal, the fowl, the fish, the reptile, the insect, the plants and minerals. "For we know that the whole creation groans and travails in pain together until now," it says in Romans 8:22.

But even before that, at the very foundations — the planning and groundwork of the whole of creation — God in His grace had a plan of salvation not just for sinful man but for innocent creation. God himself would take on a human body and give it like an innocent lamb as an atonement for man's sin. This is the Gospel message of the cross. God buying back [redeeming] that which was lost with His own blood.

In Revelation 13:8 Jesus is referred to as "The Lamb slain from the foundation of the world." We know that Jesus Christ of Nazareth was crucified about 2000 years ago fulfilling the promised remedy of Adam's transgression and sin curse we read about in the opening chapters of our Bible. John 3:16 is truly golden for us who believe: "For God so loved the world that He gave His only begotten son that whosoever believeth in Him shall not perish but have everlasting life."

And could it get better?

The Bible says "That if thou shalt confess with thy mouth the Lord Jesus and shalt believe in thine heart that God hath raised him from the dead, thou shalt be saved." Romans 10:9.

CHAPTER 13

The Great Catching Away

Recently, Janell and I caught the latest "Left Behind" film with Nicholas Cage at the local movie theater. I give it a "raving" review -- tense, and well-done. It depicted the "rapture" in a matter-of-factly kind of way showing how believers and innocent children will suddenly be "caught away" or "snatched' from the earth. The movie shows how things could play out in the immediate hours following the event, and how those "left behind" process the event that they had been told would happen. There were school buses, trucks, cars motor- cycles and planes missing passengers, pilots and drivers. In fact, much of the movie was centered on the plight of a flight. But there was at least one scene that bothered me and runs counter of the way I think it will play out.

The scene was of a beautiful and loyal black lab (I think it was a lab) sitting sorrowfully next to a hump of what we were to believe his master's clothing. "Hmm," I murmured lightly and elbowed Janell. You see, I believe a dog like that, and a dog like Sadie surely are going with their masters in the rapture (or at the very least some kind of arrangement).

I cannot prove it from direct scripture, but I can look at God's nature and his history of preservation and provision for animals just before other judgements impacting humans and creation were to occur.

The rapture, of course directly precedes the pouring out of God's wrath on a Christ-rejecting world. Jesus says in Matthew 24:21 "For then shall be great tribulation, such as was not since the beginning of the world to this time, no, nor ever shall be."

'Google' the word "rapture" you will find it is a term in Christian eschatology which refers to "being caught up" discussed in the New Testament's 1 Thessalonians 4:16, when the "dead in Christ" and "we who are alive and remain" will be "caught up in the clouds" to meet "the Lord in the air."

People will argue that the word 'rapture' is not in the Bible. That's not true. The argument that could be won is one that says the word is not in the older English translations of the Bible. But even the concept of the rapture is definitely and clearly there as we will see. It's true that if you open your King James version of the Bible and search for the word "rapture" you won't find it except in someone's footnotes. You may be surprised to learn that searching for the word "trinity" will net the same results. But both doctrines clearly come directly from scripture.

The New Testament was originally written in Greek. Many of the early Christians lived in the Roman Empire where Latin was the language. The New Testament began to be translated from Greek into Latin and the word for "caught up" is like the English word "rapture" we use today.

The Bible does not tell us exactly when but it does tell us exactly that Christ is returning one day for His church. There is debate about the event. Some teach that instead of a rapture there is a general resurrection and general judgement. This author believes God's Word is not confusing and should be taken literally where it is presented so. [See earlier explanation of premillennialism].

The Rapture will begin with Christ resurrecting the bodies of believers who have already died. Scripture teaches us that when a Christian dies, their soul goes immediately to be with the Lord while their body remains behind. Jesus told the thief on the cross, 'Today thou shalt be with Me in paradise.' — Luke 23:43. We note that the soul of the thief was with Christ, but not his body. His soul has been with Jesus since that very day and, along with countless others who have joined them the past two millennia is going to return with the Lord. The man's body is going to be raised by our Lord. His soul is going to return to a glorified body.

Of course immediately after the resurrection of believers who had passed, the rapture of living saints takes place. Again we read in 1 Thessalonians 4:17 "Then we which are alive and remain shall be caught up (raptured) together with them in the clouds, to meet the Lord in the air: and so shall we ever be with the Lord."

Jesus said: "For God so loved the world, that he gave his only begotten Son, that whosoever believeth in him should not perish, but have everlasting life." — John 3:16.

Two thousand years ago Jesus came to this world in the form of a baby born of a Virgin who had been conceived by the Holy Spirit. He did so that He might obtain a human body and die on the cross.

We call this the 1st Coming or 1st Advent (coming) of Christ.

Here is an interesting thing (what we would call in the newspaper business, a sidebar). Again. I reference Alcorn who identifies Adam, Noah and Jesus as the three heads of the three earths. When Adam was created God surrounded him with animals; when Noah was delivered, God surrounded him with animals; when Jesus was born, God surrounded Him with animals. Would it not follow that in a restored, redeemed creation animals will surround new man and new woman in a new Heaven and on a new earth?

In the book of Revelation we find "living creatures" around the throne worshipping God day and night. After the Battle of Armageddon, Jesus will establish a literal physical Millennial Kingdom where "The wolf also shall dwell with the lamb, and the leopard shall lie down with the kid; and the calf and the young lion and the fatling together; and a little child shall lead them."

— Isaiah 11:6

As for my hypothesis on dogs and other pets being raptured or resurrected along with their Bible-believing masters, I admit I am absent a direct quotable Bible verse that says "along with their beagle hounds" but I do know I am safe in concluding that a restored paradise as outlined in literal interpretation of the Bible does include animals.

Dictionaries define the word this way: rapture | ☐rapCHər | noun (the Rapture) N. Amer. (according to some millenarian teaching) the transporting of believers to heaven at the Second Coming of Christ. ORIGIN late 16th cent. (in the sense 'seizing and carrying off'): from obsolete French, or from medieval Latin raptura 'seizing,' influenced by rapt.

A look at the scriptures that relate to animals and what is said of them:

Ecclesiastes 3:18-21: "As for humans, God tests them so that they may see that they are like the animals. Surely the fate of human beings is like that of the animals; the same fate awaits them both: As one dies, so dies the other. All have the same breath (literally "spirit"); humans have no advantage over animals. Everything is meaningless. All go to the same place; all come from dust, and to dust all return. Who knows if the human spirit rises upward and if the spirit of the animal goes down into the earth?" *NIV

Job 12:10 "In whose hand is the soul of every living thing, and the breath of all mankind."

Genesis 9:9-10 "I now establish my covenant with you and with your seed after you and with every living creature that is with you—the birds, the livestock and all the animals, all those that came out of the ark with you—every living creature on earth." KJV/NIV

Genesis 9:16 "Whenever the rainbow appears in the clouds, I will see it and remember the everlasting covenant between God and all living creatures of every kind on the earth."

Genesis 6:19-22 "You are to bring into the ark two of all living creatures, male and female, to keep them alive with you. Two of every kind of bird, of every kind of animal and of every kind of creature that moves along the ground will come to you to be kept alive. You are to take every kind of food that is to be eaten and store it away as food for you and for them." Noah did everything just as God commanded him."

Genesis 1:30 "And to all the beasts of the earth and all the birds in the sky and all the creatures that move along the ground—everything that has the breath of life [spirit] in it—I give every green plant for food."

Hosea 2:18 "In that day I will make a covenant for them with the beasts of the field, the birds in the sky and the creatures that move along the ground. Bow and sword and battle will abolish from the land, so that all may lie down in safety."

*Note: The author's preferred version of the Bible is King James but yielded to editors for cause of what they call modern readability.

CHAPTER 14

New Body in New Abode

So do dogs get new bodies? And will they all be beagles. And what about rewards? And will there be any dogs in Hell? If we say that along with humans, animals are going to populate a coming kingdom and then the New Heaven and New Earth [and I believe we have already produced the scriptural evidence] then the logic follows that like humans in restored physical bodies that last forever, animals too must have such.

Remember so many of our questions are easily answered when we go back to God's original creation. That is what we are talking about. The main things present now and on earth since the Fall of Man and his departure from The Garden of Paradise will be missing in the New Paradise. They are things that defile, pollute, corrupt, pervert and kill. To answer many questions we may have about the afterlife of animals we simply study the afterlife of redeemed humans.

We trust you have read the previous chapters and understand the Dispensation [era] of Grace.

Of course, Sadie may not understand all about Heaven. In fact it would take many devoted hours in several lifetimes for just humans to get a good understanding of Heaven. Paul the Apostle writes in II Corinthians 12:2 about an experience he had possibly outside the city of Lystra in central Anatolia, now part of present-day Turkey. A mob had stoned him to death. At least those with him thought him dead [see Acts 14:19]. The Apostle got a preview of Heaven. He writes: "I knew a man in Christ fourteen years ago, (whether in the body, I cannot tell; or whether out of the body, I cannot tell: God knows;) such a one caught up to the third heaven." And from GOD'S WORD® Translation "was snatched away to paradise where he heard things that can't be expressed in words, things that humans cannot put into words. I don't know whether this happened to him physically or spiritually. Only God knows."

Last year on a December Monday after a full day of cold rain and beneath a cloud-filled sky, as part of our almost daily ritual Sadie and I drove out to Lake Sahoma to watch the sun set. [Seems we go to Liberty Park every morning and then to one of our area lakes in the evening.] Granny goes with us most evenings and takes some wonder- ful pictures of the sun setting through the clouds or reflecting off the water. We've seen some pretty ones there.

Prospects seemed "dim" that we would see much more than a gradual darkening this evening. We left her chatting on the phone and face-booking. Sadie knew it was time for the nightly. She had already slept away most of the afternoon in the front, then back seats of the pickup. She loves to do that, especially when it's cool and cloudy or raining.

As we rounded the corner and headed up 97 Highway, there it was in all of its brilliance. That beautiful star we call the sun -- the ball of fire that God created "to rule the day" coming through at first part of the clouds and then right beneath an opening to offer one of the most beautiful sunsets I have ever witnessed. I called Janell from the handsfree and told her what she was missing.

"Look Sadie, look. This is going to be glorious."

When I say to Sadie, "look" she does look but seldom in the direction I am directing. She scans the trees and ditches looking for . . . well rabbits, tree or ground. She's a beagle, after all.

"That's what I believe Heaven looks like," Sadie.

Our previous conversations about Heaven were usually distract- ed by questions about vermin, grass and trees — parks and lake shorelines and streams and smells and what we might eat once we got there. "Will there be squirrels in heaven?" she had asked.

"Yes," I would answer "and bass in lakes, trout in streams and . . ."

But with that sunset I was wanting Sadie to see all of the beauty that will be in Heaven. Human words cannot describe Heaven but a sunset comes close. The beloved Apostle John exiled on the prison Isle of Patmos records sights and sounds of Heaven for us in Revelation 4: "After this I looked, and, behold, a door was opened in heaven: and the first voice which I heard was as it were of a trumpet talking with me; which said, Come up hither, and I will shew thee things which must be hereafter. And immediately I was in the spirit: and, behold, a throne was set in heaven, and one sat on the throne. And he that sat was to look upon like a jasper and a sardine stone: and there was a rainbow round about the throne, in sight like unto an emerald. And round about the throne were four and twenty seats: and upon the seats I saw four and twenty elders sitting, clothed in white raiment; and they had on their heads crowns of gold. And out of the throne proceeded lightnings and thunderings and voices: and there were seven lamps of fire burning before the throne . . ." [1-4].

Erase your minds of that silly and typical picture of people with halos or garlands laying around on clouds, wearing wings, and play- ing harps.

Do you want to get a glimpse of Heaven? I challenge you to read the complete chapter of Revelation 21: "And I saw a new heaven and a new earth: for the first heaven and the first earth were passed away; and there was no more sea. And I, John saw the holy city, new Jerusalem, coming down from God out of heaven, prepared as a bride adorned for her husband.

"And I heard a great voice out of heaven saying, Behold, the tabernacle of God is with men, and he will dwell with them, and they shall be his people, and God himself shall be with them, and be their God. And God shall wipe away all tears from their eyes; and there shall be no more death, neither sorrow, nor crying, neither shall there be any more pain: for the former things are passed away.

"And he that sat upon the throne said, Behold, I make all things new. And he said unto me, Write: for these words are true and faithful. And he said unto me, It is done. I am Alpha and Omega, the beginning and the end. I will give unto him that is athirst of the fountain of the water of life freely. He that overcometh shall inherit all things; and I will be his God, and he shall be my son."

IN THE SPRING

From a journal entry earlier this year: (2015)

"It was damp this morning at the Park, but not that cold. Squirrels were running everywhere and scents of moles oozing from the ground. One time 'round the park was enough for the master but Sadie was not ready to go home at all. Being obedient to the master's call is abandoned. The park holds all the interest. I exit the truck and sit on a nearby park bench trying to coax Sadie to go for a squirrel she has been stalking.

"There's a greater park than this awaiting us Sadie," I tell her. She turns and looks at me. "Load up" (a command she understands as 'get in the truck or boat.') "Let's go home."

Some day we will hear a heavenly command like that and indeed we will "load up" with the Master and go Home. I have proba- bly referenced this scripture several times in this book, but it is among my favorite:" Let not your heart be troubled: ye believe in God, believe also in me. In my Father's house are many mansions: if it were not so, I would have told you. I go to prepare a place for you. And if I go and prepare a place for you, I will come again, and receive you unto myself; that where I am, there ye may be also. — John 4:1-3.

Sadie [now five in 2018] in top of picture waits for the photo session to end so she can again have attention of Harmony, 12, and Bella, 5. Sadie, who would be about 35 in dog years, grew up with these two. She also has great relationship with our other grendchildren and great GC.

CHAPTER 15

Waiting and Watching

Went to a funeral today of a friend not much older than myself. All my friends seem to be leaving this planet. Sadie waited in the truck at home. I took the old 1966 Chevy II station wagon. Permissible. The truck seldom leaves the yard without Sadie. Did I tell you she's spoiled?

Many a time, I take her with me wherever I go, and she waits in the truck in the parking lot without fuss -- except at Westlakes and Atwoods. She knows those stores are pet-friendly so when we pull up she immediately crawls into my lap with her nose solid against the door in the proximity of the handle awaiting the leash to snap.

At other times she remains perched on the center console looking at me for some instruction.

"Am I going with you master? What's up?" "Just wait for me," I tell her.

As I headed out to the funeral, I had opened the door and allowed Sadie into the truck on her leash with the usual instruction.

"Gotta go say goodbye to a friend, Sadie. I'll be back soon."

thought of my Master's promise to his followers.

At the funeral, I wondered about my friend's pets. How did he say goodbye to them? One has to wonder his last thoughts as he draped his hand down to them from the recliner that he seldom left. The days of their jumping into his lap had been curtailed. He had a condition determined to be "terminal." [All of us have such a condition]. Of course we had prayed for his healing but the portals of glory beckoned.

One day we're going. Or one day Jesus is coming for us.

What are we to do? We're to be waiting and watching.

"Even so, you too, when you see these things happening, recognize that He is near, even at the door. Look up, your redemption draweth near." — Luke 21:28

"So will all the dogs in Heaven look like me LM?" Sadie asks. "Will we all be the same size and color? How will you recognize me? And how will I recognize you?"

"Well, Sadie, those are pretty interesting questions. The Bible tells us that humans will be known there as they were known here and so will Granny and I. So, yes if the same principle applies for animals (and I am advancing that idea here) I expect you will still be a Beagle!

Of humans, the Bible says we will have new bodies with perfect hearing and eyesight and actually hear and see each other better than ever. The afflictions of the sin curse will be gone. My recently departed friend will have his healing. And we're just talking about the physical aspects! It's going to be glorious.

"Sadie, I haven't seen 'Old Deep Bark' for awhile. Wonder if his family has moved or if he's OK?"

We do not know the names of most of the dogs we meet as we take our daily treks to Liberty Park, so we give them names. Old Deep Bark is [or was] the big shaggy dog on the corner that walked rather slow and didn't have a lot of enthusiasm when he barked. But I could tell there was a day before mundane fenced back yards, chains, ropes, old dog houses and crippling joint aches he could run around the Liberty walking trail with the best of them.

"LM, are you talking about Old Deep Bark or yourself."

"A little of both, Sadie," I answer. "In fact, if you want to get the most out of a book like this you need to read between the lines."

"Surely his bark is worse than his bite," I told Sadie when we first met Old Deep Bark. He sounds like an old man with a cold."

Sadie taunts with a laugh. I hope I have won the argument about dogs laughing and crying. By the way, it's OK to cry at the passing of a saved loved one even though we realize we will be together again some sweeter day — and at the passing of a pet. I really cried when our cat Butterscotch died. I hope Old Deep Bark is OK.

• • •

MOCKERS, SCOFFERS AND LAST DAYS

The Word has much to say concerning the Last Days. 2nd Peter 3:3-4, "Knowing this first, that there shall come in the last days scoffers, walking after their own lusts, And saying, Where is the promise of his coming?" Today, many even in the middle of the Bible Belt where Sadie and I live, people attack the Bible the Word of God.

Jesus, Peter, Paul and John said it would be that way. The world mocked Noah and his family as they built the Ark for the saving of humankind and the animals. Jesus said as it was in the days of Noah so shall it be at the coming of the Son of Man. They did eat, they drank, they married wives, they were given in marriage, until the day that Noe entered into the ark, and the flood came, and destroyed them all. Likewise also as it was in the days of Lot; they did eat, they drank, they bought, they sold, they planted, they builded; But the same day that Lot went out of Sodom it rained fire and brimstone from heaven, and destroyed them all." --Luke 17:26,29

Paul writes to Timothy: "This know also, that in the last days perilous times shall come. For men shall be lovers of their own selves, covetous, boasters, proud, blasphemers, disobedient to parents, unthankful, unholy, Without natural affection, trucebreakers, false accusers, incontinent, fierce, despisers of those that are good, Traitors, heady, highminded, lovers of pleasures more than lovers of God; Having a form of godliness, but denying the power thereof: from such turn away." — 2nd Timothy 3:1-5

This passage of Scripture is proved every day here in the Tulsa, Oklahoma area. As this book goes to press in the middle of July 2015, Tulsa detectives have their 36th murder to investigate. Over in Broken Arrow, a horrific crime in one of that community's nice neighborhoods. Two teenaged brothers have been arrested [since, tried and found guilty] for the brutal murders of their parents and three of their younger siblings. One sister survived the savage hatchet and knife attacks to tell police "my brothers did this." She evidently made the 911 call.

Surely, we're living in the last of the last days before our Savior returns to rescue us from a world destined to get even worse.

CHAPTER 16

Living in the Here and Now

I don't think Sadie really wants to catch squirrels even though she looks like she's giving it her best effort. I know for a fact she can. I experienced a couple of episodes, and I'm not sure either of us are the better for it. I know that squirrel isn't. When I told my sister Evelyn and Brother Bogie [both long-time dog lovers who are probably surprised at how attached I am to a dog] what had happened they reminded me "that's just her nature."

Maybe so, but one day I sensed that Sadie was not all that hep about catching a squirrel.

"Why is that Sadie? I know you were close enough to nab that bushy tail, and you stopped in your tracks as if you wanted to give him one more chance."

"Well LM, I know you think I'm a little scared and wonder if I really want to encounter those teeth. And I can tell you -- and you should appreciate this -- I have gotten close enough to see those teeth. Let's just say, if I caught one and shook the life out of it the way I did that little gopher that one day, why LM, I'm afraid -- not of the squirrel's teeth -- but that my confidence would be such that I would catch and destroy every squirrel in Liberty Park. Then one day, we'd show up here and you would let me out of my rolling dog house and sud- denly I would have no more squirrels to chase."

"Sadie, what wisdom," I say. "You are a true conservationist."

"Well I'm glad about that LM, 'cause the way you go on some- times I can tell you don't hold liberals in very high regard."

"Sadie! Language lesson time again. I did not say conservative. I said conservationist. Two different things . . . well maybe not to- tally. And in the liberal vs. conservative debate, Sadie, it's hard to tell the difference sometimes. There are those who preach tolerance but in truth cannot tolerate any thought that does not line up with theirs. Hypocrites. It makes the hair stand up on the back of my neck."

"Really, LM? Well I can identify with that. There are things that just naturally make the hair go up on the back of my neck too. Take that big, pit-looking dog that comes through here leashed up tight to that mean-talking human. I wonder if those two are . . . what's that word, LM? hypocrites?"

"Yeah, I suspect so. But Sadie, you are doing way too much pro- filing for a pooch. I have learned one thing in this -- I'm going to be more careful in the way I describe folks around you. Sometimes, we 'all-grown-up' humans seem to forget who's listening to our words and monitoring our thoughts. Remind me to tell you about that Bible verse sometime that talks about the words of our mouth and the intents of our hearts."

"I will, LM. Does this mean it's time to go?" Sadie asks.

"Yep, load up. You've done some good chasing today. All the squirrels are up the trees. Ferdo and Fido [the two dogs that live on the southeast corner of the park] got some exercise and bark practice. I'm ready for breakfast and devotion time with Granny. And I know you are thirsty."

"Yeah, LM, and I am really glad you think I am a good conservationist."

"You are, Sadie, and a good conversationalist as well!"

Walking with, and talking to the Lord while we await his appearing is life in the hear and now. Life really is relational — with our spouses, siblings, brothers and sisters in the Lord; with our pets; and with strangers.

"Master, why did you let that dog bite me?" Sadie asked me one morning after a confrontation with another dog.

"Well, Sadie, I may be your master, but I am not the Master. I did not know she was going to act that way. And she didn't actually bite you. She tried to bite you."

"Same difference, master."

"Yeah, I know. And I appreciate how fast you are to get away from sharp teeth. Just like the other night when you were trying to get that coon out from the wheel well of the camper. Remember how I punched it with that stick? I am always rescuing you."

"Now, why did you have to bring that up?" master. "We were talking about that furry little heifer that tried to bite me in the park this morning."

"Well Sadie, to start with, she is not a heifer which would be a young cow. [I swear you are starting to pick up a lot of my language]. She was a female dog . . . eh, eh, eh, we're not even going there.

"Okay, LM. I got it. So why did that dog try to bite me? My tail was wagging, I was friendly and smiling . . . All I wanted to do was exchange some sniffs and frolics . . . Is that so wrong?"

"Good night, Sadie. Probably not so wrong, but here's our lesson today. Everyone, dog or human, is not going to receive you in the same way. Sometimes you just have to give others some space.

"I must say, you usually have better discernment. The other day when we were at Atwoods and I was checking out at the register what did you do? You started greeting the customers like you were the Atwood dog or something. And how did you do it? Why you laid down in the floor and turned your belly straight to Heaven and they couldn't resist you. Now perhaps that is the way you should have approached that dog and her owner in the park."

"We've talked about waiting and watching. Maybe we need to talk about another 'w' word — witnessing. The Bible says we are to "sanctify Christ as Lord in our hearts, always being ready to make a defense to everyone who asks to give an account for the hope that is in us, yet with gentleness and respect. — 1st Peter 3:15 NASB, et al.

"You know, Sadie, I have had some of those heifer experiences."

"Eh, eh, eh, master."

"Got it. Anyway, this 'woman' didn't like the way I was taking pictures and writing stories and she told me so. It really aggravated me. In retrospect after talking to you I think what I should have done is just laid down in the floor, stuck my belly up and begged for some scratching."

"Master, would they have let your favorite dog of all time — the one who's going with you in the rapture — visit you in jail?"

Probably not, Sadie, but the point I want to make is this: that dog treating you the way it did in the park was probably good for you — good for both of us. It showed us that from here until Jesus comes and gets us, or until we go to where He is, we will have conflicts. We will meet people who just don't like us. They don't like anything about us. They don't like the way we look, they don't like the way we smell, they don't like our singing, our howling, our picture- taking — any-thing.

"What we have to do . . ."

"I know LM, show them our bellies and move on."

"Close, Sadie, real close."

"Actually, Sadie, every experience we have teaches us things in life if we let it. The sad thing is that sometimes it takes us so long to learn.

"Are you talking 'bout my digging again, LM?"

"Well kind of . . . re-member that song I sung to you the other day about 'Old Five and Dimers'?

"Well LM, since you brought it up, can I tell you something without hurting your feelings? Your singing is OK I suppose but that fiddle thing hurts my ears. And that sound I make when you play the fiddle isn't as you seem to suggest — me singing. It's me begging for mercy."

"Alright, I got it. Are you trying to be funny again? I also just got an idea. How about every time you dig, I go get the fiddle and play for you?"

"Anyway, that Billy Joe Shaver song so fits me. I love the opening words: 'I've spent a lifetime making up my mind to be the measure of what I thought others could see . . .' then something about Cadillac buyers and Old Five and Dimers Like Me.

"Did I tell you that the writer of that song had a terrible life — drugs, alcohol, anger — but then one day he met Jesus and Savior Jesus rescued him. Amazingly, the Lord can take away the bad things and experiences and lead us in His way.

"He's a good Master, Sadie."

"And you know what, Sadie? I think some of the things you and I have discussed here will really be a blessing to some people. Why, we are very liable to meet some of our readers one day up there — along with their pets."

CHAPTER 17

Will You Be There?

So as we have already said, we may not be able to be "dog"matic about dogs having souls or that animals will be raptured and resurrected when Jesus comes again. But Sadie and I believe there is ample evidence that we will share an eternal future.

The sad part would be that someone's pet goes into the kingdom but cannot find its master who made no preparation for the journey. Like the foolish virgins in Jesus' parable who were not ready when the Bridegroom came, they have no oil in their lamps to light the way.

I know "good" people who love animals and love people. But they are in danger because they have the wrong understanding about what it takes to get to Heaven. Some folk think it is by being religious.

Others think it is by being good. They rationalize that God is going to judge us on our merit and at the end of our lives if we have done more good things than bad things we will be allowed into God's Heaven. That is the second biggest lie the Enemy has in his bag of deceptions. [We covered the biggest lie earlier when he cast doubt on God's Word and deceived Eve].

The New Testament teaches that our entrance into Heaven can never be gained by "works of righteousness that we have done" but only by the finished work of Christ on Calvary.

The Word of God says we must look "unto Jesus the author and finisher of our faith; who for the joy that was set before him endured the cross, despising the shame, and is set down at the right hand of the throne of God." — Hebrews 12:2. Further: "For by grace are ye saved through faith; and that not of yourselves: it is the gift of God: Not of works, lest any man should boast." — Ephesians 2:8-9.

Jesus said "Verily, verily, I say unto you, He that entereth not by the door into the sheepfold, but climbeth up some other way, the same is a thief and a robber." And in 14:6 "Jesus saith unto him, I am the way, the truth, and the life: no man cometh unto the Father, but by me."

When I was doing research for this book on the Internet I ran across a blog by Tom Waldron. He is the author of a book similar to this one entitled, "Will I See Him Again." He is writing about his pet cat, "Butchie." In the article [and perhaps excerpted from his book] he raises the following issue:

"So your pets will live again! But Will they see you there?" he asks. "Can you imagine your little buddy anxiously waiting in the glorious presence of our Creator for you to arrive? Only you never do? For now, he sits there waiting and watching to welcome you back home -- just like old times. But, sooner or later, he'll finally under- stand and he'll just turn and walk away -- without you -- while you spend your eternity somewhere else -- far, far away. Think about it. Just because your pets may live again, doesn't mean that you will."

If you're not sure where you will spend eternity, why don't you just now simply invite Christ into your heart and life as savior and lord. He will forgive your sins and give you a new heart and you will be rapture ready. "Behold, I stand at the door, and knock: if any man hear my voice, and open the door, I will come in to him, and will sup with him, and he with me." — Revelation 3:20.

Let Sadie and I know if you have that great question settled, and we will count on seeing you in the air or over there.

Master Don and Sadie have differing views about the music that comes from the master's fiddle!

CHAPTER 18

Some Final Thoughts

There's the "Old Yeller" book and movie; the "Ol' Shep" story and song; and of course, "Lassie" on black and white television. These were lore for dog lovers like us when we were kids and probably some of why we get emotionally connected to our own dogs today. There does seem to be something to that claim about a dog being a "man's best friend."

So it is with "Hachi" the wonderful and impacting story told in books, movies and countless news articles based on a true story. It is a heart-wrenching account of a dog and his master — more precisely the dog's loyalty and (can we say) faith? Actually, Hachikō in Japanese — hachi meaning eight, and a suffix kō meaning affection — was an Akita, a large breed dog, who lived in Shibuya, Japan from 1923-1935. The story has been written and re-written, and scripted for at least a couple of movies including the most recent "Hachi, A Dog's Tale" starring Richard Gere in 2009.

The movie is set in America although the true story played out in Japan. The hero of the story of course is Hachiko who always will be remembered because of his remarkable loyalty to his master. That loyalty continued long after his master died — actually until Hachiko himself died.

In 1924, Hidesaburō Ueno, a professor took Hachikō, as a pet. During his owner's life, Hachikō saw his master off to work and greeted him again at the end of each day at the Shibuya Station near their home.

The pair continued that daily routine until May 1925, when Professor Ueno did not return. The professor had suffered a cerebral hemorrhage and died. Each day for the next nine years, nine months and fifteen days, according to the original work, Hachikō waited for Ueno's return, showing up exactly when the train was due at the station.

In the American version of the story, Gere is Professor Parker Wilson. He finds the puppy at the station after it escaped from a broken crate in which it was being shipped from Japan to the U.S. The station manager does not want to house the dog overnight so Parker agrees to take it home while efforts are made to find its intended owner.

Wilson's wife, Cate, does not want them to keep the puppy. Parker learns the dog's breed and the next day smuggles the puppy onto the train and takes him to the university where a Japanese professor reveals that the symbol on the collar is 'Hachi' — Japanese for the number 8. It means "good fortune" he said. Parker begins calling the dog Hachiko.

At home, when Parker attempts to play fetch with Hachiko, the dog refuses. Cate is shown receiving a phone call from someone that has heard about the found puppy. They want to adopt it. The wife, looking out the window and seeing her husband playing with the pup tells the caller that it already has found a home. The bonding of two hearts is evident. Parker, who down on all fours has even demonstrated how it is done, remains perplexed by Hachiko's refusal to chase and fetch. The constant, however, is that every morning even as Hachiko grows to adulthood, he accompanies his master to the train station, and every evening is there again when the master returns home — save the one afternoon when Hachiko was blocked by a skunk. The professor had grown accustomed to looking out the window as the train approached the station and seeing his faithful dog waiting for him. He was alarmed that afternoon not to see Hachiko in his usual spot. Soon the frantic professor was searching for and finally rescuing his dog from the skunk.

One morning, Parker prepares to leave for work but Hachiko protests with loud barking. The professor heads out to the station and soon Hachiko follows with that ball in his mouth. Parker is surprised but pleased that Hachiko is finally willing to play fetch with him. A couple of throws and then Parker catches his train despite more barking. Later that day Parker is teaching, still holding Hachi's ball, when he suddenly grabs his chest, falls to the floor and dies. At the train station, Hachiko waits patiently as the train arrives, but his master does not appear through the doors. After several hours wait- ing in the snow, a family member finds the dog and takes him home.

The next day, Hachiko returns to the station and waits. Family members can't contain the dog. He waits for his master every day, while at night sleeping in the rail yard. The broken-hearted dog is befriended by the cart vendor who had given Professor Wilson his coffee every morning. Hachiko's loyalty is soon featured in the local newspaper and wins national attention.

The professor's wife, Cate, had sold the house and moved away. Years had passed and she returns to visit Parker's grave on the anniversary of his death. She is astonished to see Hachiko maintaining his vigil at the train station. Grief-stricken, she embraces the old family friend and then sits and waits for the next train with him.

Now, here's the super good part depicted in both, the 1980s Japanese movie and in the 2009 American movie: Hachiko had continued his daily walk to the same spot in front of the train station to his final day. There he was, visibly old and slow. He arrives at the spot where he last saw his master and recollects their lives together. There he lays himself down and closes his eyes. He then imagines Parker coming out of the station and the two greeting each other. There's a bright light as the professor comes reaching out to his beloved dog.

Film reviewers rightly interpret that closing scene as Hachiko dying and reuniting with his beloved master in Heaven. In the movie, Hachiko is last seen lying on the snow, alone and still.

What a perfect picture of what we've tried to relate in this book. Pets as much as their masters want to be eternally together. Of course, dogs aren't human. They won't ever be. They won't become angels. But the faith and loyalty of God's creatures demonstrated during their earthly existence isn't to be winked at nor will those qualities go unrewarded. Who do you think puts such things in the heart of a mere dog? We as humans know much about our creator by considering His creatures.

As stated at the beginning of this labor of love, I admit I cannot give you scripture that absolutely says pets will be raptured (transported) to Heaven alone or at the same time as their believing humans. I cannot dogmatically tell you that animals will be raptured or resurrected, but I can show you the heart of Our Master in the way he disperses love, faith and eternity. When we attend to that it is harder still to reconcile a Heaven and future kingdom without animals — especially our faithful companions.

In the Gospel of John we find Jesus explaining to his followers that he is going away — back to Heaven — and how his death, burial and resurrection will play out ultimately.

"Let not your heart be troubled," he told them. "You believe in God, believe also in me. In my Father's house are many mansions: if it were not so, I would have told you. I go to prepare a place for you. And if I go and prepare a place for you, I will come again, and receive you unto myself; that where I am, there ye may be also." I believe Jesus is talking about a his physical return to this physical earth from a physical Heaven. In the Book of Acts 1:11 we have the question: "Ye men of Galilee, why stand ye gazing up into heaven? this same Jesus, which is taken up from you into heaven, shall so come in like manner as ye have seen him go into heaven."

However "redemption" is understood, be assured that for the Bible believer, it means restoration and reunion. When we say "day of redemption" we are referring to a salvation that includes future glorification of fleshly abodes. Being with our Creator. When I saw the presentation of the Professor returning for Hachiko I was remind- ed of scripture. "For our citizenship is in heaven, from which also we eagerly wait for a Savior, the Lord Jesus Christ; 21 who will transform the body of our humble state into conformity with the body of His glory, by the exertion of the power that He has even to subject all things to Himself."— Phil. 3:20-21. "And He is the image of the invisible God, the first-born of all creation." — Col. 1:15

Many times we understand "loved ones" to be our human family members or other believers. I hope I am not understood to be elevating animals above humans, but I do believe that the love between humans and their companion pets is divinely sparked.

"So now faith, hope, and love abide, these three; but the greatest of these is love," — 1st Cor. 13.

The purpose of this book is to give assurance that love is eternal and we who love God can expect to see out pets in Heaven. And should the Lord return while we are still alive, "we shall be caught up together with them in the clouds, to meet the Lord in the air: and so shall we ever be with the Lord." — 1st Thes. 4:17

After his death in 1935, Hachikō's remains were cremated and his ashes were buried alongside those of his beloved master. Hachikō's fur was preserved, stuffed and mounted as a permanent display at Japan's Natural Science Museum in Tokyo. In April 1934, a bronze statue in his likeness was erected at Shibuya Station. Hachikō himself was present at its unveiling. The statue was recycled for the war effort during World War II but in 1948 a new statue was erected and today is a popular meeting spot. The station entrance where Hachiko waited and watched is nearby. The exact spot where Hachikō waited in the train station is marked with bronze paw-prints. In November 2015, the very time final drafts of this manuscript was taking place, a previously undiscovered photograph of Hachikō was published for the first time. The image, which was captured in 1934 by a Tokyo bank employee, shows the dog relaxing in front of Shibuya Station.

Addendum and Update:

Since writing the "Sadie Book" three years ago I stumbled upon another great true dog story that I want to recommend: "Jim The Wonder Dog" by Clarence Dewey Mitchell.

I should have remembered. I first learned of Jim when I was working as a reporter for the Daily Democrat News years ago in Marshall, Mo. (on U.S. 65 just north of I-70 between Kansas City and Columbia).

Last year when we were through there for a visit, we stopped at a beautiful downtown park and museum dedicated to the famous dog. The park had been built since I moved from Marshall in the late 1970s. Our paper had ran the story of Jim from time to time in special editions. His grave in the local cemetery was the most visited.

Initially, however, authorities did not allow Jim to be buried in the cemetery but just outside the fence. Ironically, the cemetery has expanded and now Jim's grave, according to one source, "is right in the middle of it."

Famous for a couple of uncanny phenomenons displayed by the animal, Jim lived from 1925 into the mid-1930s (1937). Not only was he the subject of features in the local newspaper, but in the Kansas City Star, the St. Louis Post-Dispatch, etc., and the likes of Outdoor Life Magazine.

Jim performed before the Missouri Legislature and at the Missouri State Fair in Sedalia. He was studied and written about at the University of Missouri School of Veterinary Medicine. Newspaper and magazine writers came to a hotel in Marshall from all over to witness the dog's incredulous feats and then write of them. Jim's fame spread across the United States and beyond. He was featured regularly in Ripley's Believe It or Not newspaper feature. A book penned in the dog's voice by Clarence Dewey Mitchell simply entitled "Jim The Wonder Dog" is an absolute page-turner. One of the people who more recently wrote of Jim and helped memorialize him is the late Evelyn Counts. Her writings revived the earlier story of the black and white sitter that had unexplainable abilities including carrying out instructions given to him in any foreign language, shorthand, or Morse Code. He was capable of predicting the outcome of future events. He chose the winner of seven Kentucky Derbies, The World Series of baseball and the sex of unborn babies.

Counts passed in 2013 but not before the memorial garden was built for Jim, the book republished and Marshall found a renewed place of the map. Newspapers still carry the story but even the History Channel and Animal Planet have paid visits to the site of the old Hotel and the streets where Jim The Wonder Dog amazed many a human. The following comes from one of Counts' stories, "A Short Tail About Jim."

"Jim was a Llewellyn setter born of pureblood champion field stock in Louisiana," she writes. "Though his litter mates were selling for $25 each, a goodly sum in 1925, he was considered the most unlikely of the litter and came into Sam VanArsdale's hands for less than half that amount. Attempts to train Jim for the field seemed futile as he lay in the shade watching while the trainer worked with the three other dogs. However, when taken to the field that fall for the first time, he immediately went to a covey of quail, came up on perfect point, held steady until the quail was shot, and immediately brought the bird to Mr. VanArsdale on the order to "fetch." He proved to be a marvelous hunting dog, knowing where there were quail, and refusing to hunt where there were none. His master, an avid hunter who traveled from state to state hunting, kept track of birds shot over his beloved dog. He stopped counting at 5,000, a total no other dog ever reached. *Outdoor Life Magazine* termed Jim "The Hunting Dog of the Country".

However, Jim was much more than just a champion hunting dog since Mr. VanArsdale found, quite by accident while in the field one day, that his dog could understand what he was saying to him and carried out his commands. It was a hot day, and Mr. VanArsdale said, "Let's go over and rest a bit under that Hickory tree". Although in a woods of numerous kinds of trees, he went to the Hickory. Surprised by this, he asked Jim to go to a Walnut, then a Cedar, a stump, and a tin can, which he did rapidly and perfectly. This was the start of the amazing things the dog did on command. When told to do so, he could go out on the street and locate a car by make, color, out-of- state, or a license number. From a crowd he could select the "man who sells hardware", and the one who "takes care of sick people", or the "visitor from Kansas City."

In 1935 Jim performed in Wyoming at the Kemmerer Hotel. After his successful performance, an article was written in the Kemmerer Gazette, Friday, August 30, 1935, referring to Jim as "The Wonder Dog." Jim also performed before the Missouri Legislature and at the Missouri State Fair in Sedalia. Newspaper and magazine writers came to witness Jim and were stunned. They wrote of incredulous things they saw and Jim's fame spread across the United States and elsewhere. He was featured in Ripley's Believe It or Not.

The site of the Jim The Wonder Dog Garden off the northwest corner of the Square was once occupied by the Ruff Hotel where Jim lived with its managers the VanArsdales. For Marshall, the site commemorates one of it's most famous "citizens." Pay it a visit. Meanwhile check out: www.jimthewonderdog.org

. . . *Meanwhile*

stay tuned for more updates, review the book now published in paperbook by Kindle Direct Publishing on Amazon, send me your favorite dog story and follow my blogs at: "A Done Deal — The Way I See It" on Facebook

As for an update on our activities (Sadie's, mine and Granny's), we still have our daily outings. Sadie has grown in "understanding" (a term I picked up from the Jim the Wonder Dog book) and is even more "spoiled." Our list of places to go has definitely increased. She gathers and shares ticks and poison ivy from the woods around Reynolds Park and Heyburn Lake. (We have learned some great preventative measures and will be sharing on my blogs sometime).

Besides fishing and our woods adventures, we go camping and make mission trips together. We still visit Liberty Park where we had our first conversations about Heaven and then named all the neighborhood dogs. "Ferdo and Fido" have moved and "Old Gruff" may have passed. "Buddy" has gotten fatter and all of us have become older. There's a pot-bellied pig at which Sadie tries to grunt . . . and of course, some ducks, rabbits, and the squirrels.

Sadie turned five on June 1 (2018). That's equal to 35 human years. She has become a little more aggressive and barks louder than ever when she wants her way and sees I am not wearing my hearing aids. She can run 40 mph at the Creek County Fairgrounds when she stretches out while racing the pickup (which, by the way, still serves as her rolling doghouse. She also hangs out there when we're at church). We're trying to get Sadie to tolerate "kitty cats" more and to leave off attacking the o'possums that venture into our yard. They have a lot of positives including ridding your yard of ticks. Sadie's not buying it.

I have had some real good reviews on our book as well as some very pointed ridicule. Sadie and I find ourselves dividing the sheep from the goats (that's dog lovers from non-dog lovers) and agree that humans lack understanding and may tend to be more hateful than dogs on occasion.

Granny stays busy with the grandkids. We're still publishing our online newspaper [Sapulpa News & Views] and I stay busy writing. I did a book for the Sapulpa Historical Society "Sapulpa — A Pictorial History" published be Arcadia Press as part of its "Images of America Series," and am currently getting two more books ready for publication: "Invasion: Killing of the Indian" and "Viola, Stories My Mamma Told and the Songs She Sang." [or is that "sung?"]

We continue to witness for our Lord and urge people to trust Him completely, know Him and receive Him as personal Lord and Savior; not to hold on to this world too tightly but to set their affection on things above and the kingdom to come.

— Don Diehl, 2018

Made in the USA
Lexington, KY
21 September 2018